Devotionally Yours, Philippians

Devotionally Yours, Philippians

Bill Owen
Mike Smith
Tom Steagald

BROADMAN PRESS
Nashville, Tennessee

© Copyright 1980 • Broadman Press.
All rights reserved.

4251-76
ISBN: 0-8054-5176-5

Dewey Decimal Classification: 227.6
Subject headings: BIBLE. N.T. PHILIPPIANS//DEVOTIONAL
                LITERATURE

Library of Congress Catalog Card Number: 79-6023
Printed in the United States of America

Contents

Preface 9

An Opening Prayer 11

Introduction. 13

I. Salvation

Grace and Joy—A Word

   Study   1:2,4 19

The Process   1:6 21

In Whatever Happens   1:12 23

Varieties of Witness   1:15-18 25

Serving Christ   1:29 28

Cooperation   2:1-2 29

Jesus Knows Me   2:5-8 30

Work Out Your Salvation

   2:12-13 32

Right Priorities   3:7 34

The Gift of Righteousness   3:9 . . . 37

The Transforming Christ   3:21 . . . 39

II. Discipleship

Servants   1:1; 2:4 45

Saints   1:2 47

Memories 1:3 49

In Every Prayer 1:4 51

I Long for You All 1:8 53

Death . . . Life 1:20 55

Doing What's Necessary 1:21-24 . 58

Worthy Living 1:27 61

Servanthood 2:5-7 63

Bowing My Knees 2:9-11 66

Lights to the World 2:14-16 67

Holding Fast the Word of

    Life 2:16 70

Plans 2:19 73

The Interests of Christ 2:20-21 .. 75

Misplaced Zeal 3:2-7 78

Knowing 3:8-11 81

Five Finger Exercises 3:12,14-15 .. 84

Life in the Present Tense 3:13 ... 86

A Good Example 3:17-19 88

The Way to Stand Firm

    4:1-6,8-9*a* 93

The Strength of Christ 4:13 96

Abundance of Blessings 4:18-19 . 99

III. Community and Joy

    Partners 1:5 105

    Fight Together 1:27 107

    The Mercy of God 2:27 109

    Repeating the Great Truths 3:1 . . 111

    Citizens of Heaven 3:20 114

    The Peace of God 4:7,9*b* 116

    Joy in Christ 4:10-12 118

    Partners in the Gospel 4:14-17 . . . 120

    Glory to God 4:20 122

    Greetings and Grace 4:21-23 124

Preface

Paul's letter to the Philippians is unsurpassed in its value for the Christian life. It is literally packed with truths and insights into the nature and practice of Christianity. This book is designed to enable the reader to tap the abundant resources of this, Paul's most personal letter. In doing so, we hope the reader will find guidance toward living more fully in the way of the Lord Jesus Christ.

This book can be used in a variety of ways. It may be used for private devotions, as well as for devotional introduction to Philippians. Groups may also use it for common devotion or small prayer groups. Busy pastors will find illustrations and prayers, and may use it as a reference.

It is our sincere prayer that God may richly bless you as you discover the beauty of Philippians and as the Scripture opens to you new paths of Christian living. Even as we have grown and matured as we have studied and written, we hope you will experience growth and development in the life of faith.

We wish to thank our wives for their love and support—as well as patience—through the writing process. Also, to all those who gave encouragement and helpful suggestions along the way—pastors, professors, family, and friends.

And a special word of thanks to Carol Poston, our typist, who took the time to be not only our typist but to be an advisor and friend.

Bill Owen
Mike Smith
Tom Steagald

Louisville, Kentucky
October, 1979

An Opening Prayer

Heavenly Father,
Maker and Redeemer of the universe, of which
   we are a part,
Lord of life, and Saver of our souls:
We desire to feel your hand of blessing upon us.
We long to walk in your ways,
   because you made us for yourself and our hearts
   find no peace until they rest in you.

Be now our guide in this study, as we turn to your
   Word for blessings and guidance for our lives.
Lead us to your truth.
We pray with the psalmist,
   "Oh send out thy light and thy truth;
     let them lead me,
   let them bring me to thy holy hill
     and to thy dwelling" (Ps. 43:3, RSV).

And as we come to your dwelling, to that place where
   we find ourselves,
Help us also to find anew the comfort of the Spirit,
   The love of the Son, new fellowship with the saints,
And new awarenesses of you.
                 Amen.

Introduction

William Barclay, the noted English scholar, has said that the epistle to the Philippians could be called the "Epistle of Joy," or the "Epistle of Excellent Things." Without a doubt, this letter stands as an unsurpassed monument to the man, Paul, and to his love for his friends in the faith at Philippi.

Philippians is an extremely personal and intimate letter between friends of long-standing. There is a gentleness and a serenity to this letter which is not found elsewhere. In Philippians we do not read long theological passages, such as we find in Romans. Neither are we confronted with the full-blown problems and controversies which we see in the Corinthian correspondence. Paul does not have to defend his right to speak, or his authority, as he does in other letters (cf. 1 Cor. 9:1 ff. Gal. 1:11-16). Rather, there is the kind of interchange between old friends that shows us, as A. T. Robertson has said, the more "tender" side of Paul—his delicacy, his courtesy, his elevation of feeling, his independence, his mysticism, and his spiritual passion.

And yet, besides the evident joy and friendship of the letter, we can also sense that Paul was concerned about the continual well-being of the church in Philippi. While joy is the perspective from which Paul wrote, he was concerned about the grumblings and questionings which were occurring (cf. Phil. 2:14).

The Philippian letter was written after the Corinthian letters. We know that Paul had been confronted already with, and had addressed himself to, the problems which could arise in the local church setting. It is only natural to sense Paul's concern for these people. He did not want them to experience the turmoil which had gripped Corinth. He wrote with that concern in mind.

In addition, unity was a major theme of Paul's ministry. In his latter years, he was concerned with receiving an offering from the Gentile churches to help the Jerusalem church. Paul was trying to persuade the Gentile Christians to help the Jewish Christians in their need. Paul longed for unity between these two great streams within the faith. This offering was representative of that quest for unity.

So, as Paul wrote to the Philippian church, he was thinking of Corinth, and he was concerned for the unity of the church. This concern for unity was not confined only to the universal church, for Paul also longed for unity within the local church at Philippi. Any hint of discord, as there is in the epistle, spurred Paul to exhortation. There is joy and emotion and remembrance in this letter. There is also warning, for the Philippians were special to Paul.

Why? The Philippian church was so taken with the message of Christ, and they were so responsive to Paul's missionary efforts, they became Paul's "partners" in the gospel (cf. 1:5). They were a team, and each held the other in special regard. The church aided Paul in his missionary work by supporting him with their offerings. And they sent more than their money. They sent Epaphroditus to bring money and to assist Paul in his work. The Philippians' aid was unsolicited and from the heart, while Paul urged other churches to participate in the collection. Thus, the cords of love between Paul and the Philippian church were tightly intertwined and knotted together.

There is little doubt that this epistle was written

while Paul was imprisoned and awaiting trial (cf. 1:12-24). It is impossible to know the exact time or location of the writing. It is generally accepted that Paul probably wrote from Rome between the years A.D. 61 and 63. In any event, the important thing is that Paul was under arrest at the time of the writing. He was on trial for his ministry, and he faced a possible death sentence at the hands of the Roman court.

It is understandable, therefore, to sense in the letter an overflowing of emotion from Paul's heart as he wrote. Paul was growing older, the future was uncertain, and he had many fond memories of the Philippian church. Perhaps during his imprisonment, his mind once again turned to those who had been so very faithful to him over the years. Perhaps he remembered the times they were together, their joint ventures in the faith, and the mutual goals toward which they were striving.

Paul probably realized that he might never again have personal contact with this church which he loved so much. At least not direct personal contact. While he wrote he was setting his heart to come back to them and soon (1:26). But there was still the trial, and there was the very real possibility of an unfavorable verdict. That judgment could mean Paul's continued imprisonment or even his death. This prospect for death, or even lengthy imprisonment, was the very reason why all of the exhortations of this book carried a kind of finality. Philippians 1:27 underpins the whole book—Paul hoped to see them again, but he instructed them to remain faithful whether he was there or not.

The book of Philippians shows an amazing faith. Paul celebrated, he gloried, he warned, he exhorted. He hoped to see them but said farewell to them, since he was ready to die. Above all, though, he rejoiced, and it is this which makes the letter so unique. Paul had learned, in his life's struggles, that the blessing of God is the presence of joy and peace no matter what the circumstances. And we learn that lesson from this writing. Philippians tells us that no matter where we are, we may still rejoice. So to the church at Philippi he said, in effect, "No matter what happens, rejoice!" And not just to the church at Macedonia but to anyone who would draw near unto the spirit of Christianity, Paul said, "Rejoice in the Lord alway: and again I say, Rejoice" (4:4).

I
Salvation

Grace and Joy—A Word Study
1:2,4

Grace to you and peace from God our Father and the Lord Jesus Christ . . . . always in every prayer of mine for you all making my prayer with joy (1:2,4, RSV).

Have you ever heard the story about the man who physically suffered hunger, thirst, coldness, destitution, toil, vigils, beatings, stonings, imprisonments, shipwrecks, perils of robbers, sea, and wilderness? This same fellow also suffered rejection, slander, and humiliation. He suffered over the sorrow and anguish of others, as well. That's a terrible story, isn't it? That fellow was probably sorry he was ever born. If I had been him, I might have jumped in the ocean!

"Rejoice in the Lord always; again I will say, Rejoice" (4:4, RSV). What? Who said that? Who are you to be telling people always to rejoice? You must be crazy if you think that anyone could live in this day and be happy *all* the time. I get so tired of these Christians who are always "praising the Lord," always smiling, regardless of the situation. They seem insensitive to human emotions and problems. There are times when I am angry, depressed, and worried. At other times I feel like crying. I *can* rejoice—but certainly not all the time. Who are you anyway?

"My name is Paul, and again I say rejoice. But I think you have misunderstood. By the way, I am the man spoken of above. Originally, it was I who shelled out the pain. I harassed and punished every

19

Christian I found. In fact, I was a primary leader in their persecution. But, as you know, now I am a Christian, a servant of the Lord Jesus Christ. In his service I have been on the receiving end of some of the same kind of hurt I administered. I too have been angry, depressed, and worried. I have cried more times than I can remember. But I still say rejoice always in the Lord. Let me explain.

"If you have read my letters you know that I speak often of grace. 'For you know the grace of our Lord Jesus Christ, that though he was rich, yet for your sake he became poor, so that by his poverty you might become rich' (2 Cor. 8:9, RSV). 'For by grace you have been saved through faith; and this is not your own doing, it is the gift of God' (Eph. 2:8, RSV). Grace is both the giving love and forgiving love of God as evidenced in Jesus Christ's death, burial, and resurrection on our behalf."

I agree and have professed Jesus Christ as my personal Lord and Savior. But still, how could you rejoice in the midst of the suffering you experienced?

"Perhaps you can better understand by looking at the word *grace* itself. Grace (*charis*) and joy (*chara*) are intimately related. They come from the root *char*- indicating what gives pleasure or joy. The starting point is understanding the experiences of grace as being made 'glad by gifts.' So it follows, we who have received the grace of God, the greatest gift of all, ought to be people of joy. The grace of God is our joy.

"Now be sure and understand, we are not to present ourselves to the world as those who glibly smile at any situation. Joy is never simply a mood. Rather joy is closely associated with and a natural result of the grace which we have received in Jesus Christ.

"Again I say to you my friend, as one who has

rejoiced in prison and at other times of suffering, joy is not a mood but an outlook on life. Thus, whatever the circumstance—be it suffering or blessing—our perspective is one of joy. We are able to have faith in the workings of Christ in each instance, one that God is working out his will, and surer, still, that his will will always include our best interests. Sure of God's grace, we can be joyful—even when life hurts.''

May we all, because of the grace of God, understand our lot as that of purpose and joy. God grant us purpose and grace, even as we respond in love and joy.

Amen.

The Process
1:6

And so I am sure that God, who began this good work in you, will carry it on until it is finished in the Day of Christ Jesus (1:6, GNB).

Curtis will soon have his first birthday. He's a beautiful little boy. He's the son of friends of ours, and the first baby I've known all the way through. I remember when Stephanie first wrote me that she was pregnant. I remember her and Frank's excitement through the early months. I remember the showers, the parenting classes, and how each time I saw her she looked a little more pregnant.

Everything was in flux. Frank and Stephanie, especially Stephanie, were trying to adjust to new roles, new responsibilities, and new identities—both with each other and with all who knew them. They were busy readying the nursery and readying themselves. Each day held new problems, new challenges, and new depths of awareness. Meanwhile, the baby was developing in his own way, preparing for his grand debut.

Then he was born. And somehow all the preparation was not quite enough. More adjustments had to be made. Trying to imagine a 4 AM feeding was nothing compared to the real thing.

The process had not stopped. It had just begun. Curtis' growth was phenomenal, his development obvious. His parents were growing too. Learning to respond to new crises and new challenges caused them to grow as parents. New life caused new development for both Curtis and his mom and dad.

And the process which had started will never stop. Curtis will grow throughout his whole life, even as his parents will continue developing themselves. Life never allows us to stop. We never arrive. Rather, we're always on the way.

I think this story is an example for all of us as Christians. God is our Father; we are his children. God has started our new life in the Son—a "good thing," Paul called it. And God helps us develop throughout our lives as Christians. God responds to us as a parent. He celebrates when we do his will. He hurts when we hurt. He grieves when we fall short.

When Israel was a youth I loved him,
And out of Egypt I called My Son.
Yet it is I who taught Ephraim to walk,
I took them in My arms;
But they did not know that I healed them.
I led them with cords of a man, with bonds of love,
And I became to them as one who lifts the yoke
    from their jaws;
And I bent down and fed them.
How can I give you up, O Ephraim?

How can I surrender you, O Israel?
My heart is turned over within Me,
All my compassions are kindled.

(Hosea 11:1,3-4,8, NASB)

We are God's children. He will lead us on in the
paths we need to go, even as he walks along with us.
He will help us mature and grow, until he perfects us
on the day of the Lord.

Father,
Help us respond to your leading
Knowing we never arrive, but that we're always on
     the way.
Confident of your love; help us be assured that you
     are with us at every point
—rejoicing with us
—crying with us
—struggling even as we struggle
And confident we will be that as we go together
     you are preparing us for the new day and age,
Preparing us for the coming of your Son.

In whose name we pray,
Amen.

In Whatever Happens
1:12

*I want you to know, my brothers, that the things
that have happened to me have really helped the
progress of the gospel (1:12, GNB).*

Duke McCall, the president of The Southern
Baptist Theological Seminary in Louisville,
Kentucky, recently told of the only time he
remembered crying himself to sleep. He was a

student at the seminary, and his home church in Memphis had called him home to preach. It was his first sermon ever, but it did not occur to him to be nervous—not until the fellow who introduced him made it a point during his remarks to tell McCall how nervous he ought to be. And then he was.

Dr. McCall said that he totally lost what he'd planned to say, that he stammered, stuttered, and limped through his allotted time, convinced he made no sense at all.

On the Pullman back to Louisville, he cried himself to sleep.

He now muses, "They waited two years before they asked me back." But when he did go back, a lady came up to him after the service and said, "Brother McCall, do you remember your first sermon here?" McCall answered that he did, painfully. She said, "Well, some friends of mine and I were dancing to the radio that night, and the music stopped to carry this church's regular Sunday night service. And because one of the fellows there had known you in high school, he said he wanted to hear what you had to say. So I listened. And I was saved."

By Dr. McCall's own admission, God had somehow worked in spite of him. God took the stuttering and confusion of a nervous young preacher and turned it into an avenue into the kingdom for that lady. Such is the grace and power of God. God takes every situation, and works in it and through it for the advancement of the kingdom. Paul says it here, even as in Romans 8:28: "We know that in all things God works for good with those who love him, those whom he has called according to his purpose" (GNB).

Things happen which, in and of themselves, are not according to the will of the Father. God didn't want Paul to be beaten, forsaken, or nearly killed. But when those things happened, God was so dedicated to Paul that he was able to turn the bad into victory.

All things that happen can help spread the gospel if we work with God according to his purposes. We may not understand just how his will may be accomplished, but God is faithful to us, even as we are faithful to him. Even if we stammer or evil befalls us, God is able to use it toward the redemption of others, toward the redemption of the world.

Varieties of Witness
1:15-18

Of course some of them preach Christ because they are jealous and quarrelsome, but others from genuine good will. These do so from love, because they know that God has given me the work of defending the gospel. The others do not proclaim Christ sincerely, but from a spirit of selfish ambition; they think that they will make more trouble for me while I am in prison. It does not matter! I am happy about it—just so Christ is preached in every way possible, whether from wrong or right motives. And I will continue to be happy (1:15-18, GNB).

At one point in my pilgrimage as a young believer, coming to grips with my own call to ministry, I listened to gospel radio all the time. I guess I was trying to keep my mind on the "loftier" things of the Word. And having been brought up on rock-and-roll, the adjustment was a big one.

Every young preacher has to imitate other

preachers while developing his own style. I began listening very closely to the radio preachers, trying to learn not only their style and delivery but also their theology. I thought these fellows had somehow arrived—I mean, they were on radio while I listened—and I knew I needed to learn.

As I listened, I tried to identify with them—tried to plug in to what they were saying—so that I could nod my head and "amen" at the right spots. But increasingly I found that I couldn't plug in to what they were saying. Their experiences were unique to them and generally removed from my experience of grace.

Now I'm sure I'm generalizing, but it seemed to me that every one of those nationally syndicated preachers had experienced some miraculous encounters with God. They had been delivered from dope addiction or alcoholism or had been on death row at San Quentin when God saved them. They had powerful witnesses. But I had always been a "good boy," and that picture of grace did not stir me at all.

These fellows seemed to be in demand as preachers, though. And wanting to preach as badly as I did, I became jealous of them. I actually prayed to experience some kind of vision or something spectacular, so I could have that powerful, dynamic witness.

My experience, after all, was so ordinary. I was saved at an early age under my father's preaching and grew up within the context of church life. I decided during my adolescence that I would go into full-time Christian service. I had never experienced a healing or other miracle. I even had doubts about that kind of thing. I had doubts about a lot of things. But after all the doubt and skepticism, I was a believer. I loved the Lord, and I knew he loved me—as unspectacular as that may seem to some.

Then I realized there were a lot of folk just like me—folk who had never been anything but "normal" and "good." I realized that those people needed Jesus, just like I did. And to those with doubts and fears, my testimony of simple faith could be very powerful indeed. No fireworks maybe, but powerful.

As I matured as a Christian, I began to realize that it takes all of us to build the kingdom of God. I can't talk to drug-addicts very well. But there are a lot of preachers who can't talk to the upper middle class or academic community, while I can. I learned not to be jealous of others' testimonies or begrudge the fanfare of flaming evangelists, movie stars, or ex-athletes. I learned that God's activity in my life was just as special, though not as noisy, and that people needed to hear my witness.

I am thankful for my witness. My witness allows me to be an instrument of God's love to people who need it. I can now rejoice for those whose testimonies are powerfully spectacular, for they reach a whole segment of the lost and unchurched I could never approach. And after all, we're all in this together.

I have yet to reach the wisdom of Paul, though. He even said that he was thankful for those who preach for selfish reasons, without the sincere concern for the furtherance of the gospel. If Paul were alive today, he would note that there are a lot of those folk around now. He would be right. We have a lot of charlatans and con-men operating in the name of the gospel. I pray that I will be able to believe someday what Paul knew—that God's Word will often work in spite of the proclaimer; that the truth of the gospel will outshine and outlast the individual concern; that God's grace is most evident at the point of sin, even if that sin is in the speaker of the Word.

But I'm still growing.

May God grant unto me the wisdom and patience that I glory wherever the name of Christ is preached. Amen.

Serving Christ
1:29

For you have been given the privilege of serving Christ, not only by believing in him, but also by suffering for him" (1:29, GNB).

"Oh, Lord, I love you more than life. Use me now in your will—even if that will takes me to my death. You can trust me, Lord, I'm even willing to die for you."

The reply to my prayer was interesting.

"I'm glad you're willing to die for me. And your willingness shows that you really believe in me. But that doesn't mean I can trust you with great responsibility in the faith."

"But Lord . . . ."

"For me to give you great responsibility, you must greatly prove your faith to me."

"What else can I do but die for you?"

"Live for me. Death is but for a moment and can be faced with great courage. But life is for a lifetime, and for my servants, can only be faced with great faith. Living for me is harder than dying for me."

"Help me, Father, to be willing to do both—to live for you every day, and die for you if need be. Amen."

Cooperation

2:1-2

So if there is any encouragement in Christ, any incentive of love, any participation in the Spirit, any affection and sympathy, complete my joy by being of the same mind, having the same love, being in full accord and of one mind (2:1-2, RSV).

Years ago when a new Air Force base was being constructed in Texas, the specifications called for a four-mile piece of conduit to run along one side of the base. The director of the project, a very famous officer with the Corps of Engineers, had the entire length of pipe welded together while the trench was being dug. His purpose was to conserve time. The only problem was that the trench was six feet deep, and after the welding had been done, the engineer realized that they had no way of lowering that great pipe into the trench without breaking it at the weld-seams. The project was stalled for days, until one of the workers, who had been hired as an extra, suggested that ice be placed level with the ground at intervals along the trench. The pipe could then be rolled onto the ice, and as the ice melted uniformly in the Texas heat, the pipe would be lowered automatically into the trench. The engineer immediately adopted the plan, and it was successful.

It takes a great spirit of cooperation for an engineer to be willing to heed the suggestion of a worker. This kind of spirit is needed in every area of life, especially within our churches. Paul wrote to the church in Philippi about this very thing. An appeal for unity and cooperation may be the major theme of this letter. This appeal for cooperation rests upon the reality of "encouragement" which is in Christ, the "incentive" of love, "participation," in the Holy Spirit, and "affection and sympathy," in his readers.

Paul's desire was that the church stand fast and cooperate in the cause of the gospel. He began his appeal by mentioning the "encouragement," that is, the support which is ours in Christ Jesus. Literally, it is a "calling alongside." He is present with us, alongside us all the way. We can count on God's power assisting or cooperating with our own. Paul emphasized and defined this idea. The "incentive of love" speaks of Christ's love to us, reviving us when we are weary. The "participation in the Spirit" refers to the partnership we have with God through the Spirit. "Affection and sympathy" point to the compassion of the Philippians that came from their relationship to Jesus.

Thus it is overwhelmingly evident that we have in the Lord Jesus Christ one who participates with us in whatever the circumstance or situation. The lesson for us is this: God cooperates or works with us through Jesus Christ, so we are called to cooperate with one another "by being of the same mind, having the same love, being in full accord and of one mind."

Jesus Knows Me
2:5-8

Have this mind among yourselves, which is yours in Christ Jesus, who, though he was in the form of God, did not count equality with God a thing to be grasped, but emptied himself, taking the form of a servant, being born in the likeness of men. And being found in human form he humbled himself and be-

*came obedient unto death, even death on a cross
(2:5-8, RSV).*

Life is sometimes very lonely.

You know what I mean. There are days when no
one seems to understand you. Sometimes it even
seems that no one cares enough to want to try to
understand what makes you tick. On those kinds of
days, you feel isolated from the world, from
friends—even from your family. You move through
the day making small talk with the people around
you, mechanically doing your work, all the time
knowing that something is wrong. And then it dawns
on you—you recognize your problem, and you think:
I am lonely.

Even on the best of days with our best friends or
our spouse, we sense some lack of understanding.
The simple fact is that no person ever really knows all
there is to know about another person. Try as we
might, none of us can completely comprehend the
emotions, thoughts, and motives of those around us.
And so we are lonely and misunderstood to a degree.

Among the boldest claims of the Christian faith is
the assertion that Jesus Christ understands us. God
became a human being in the person of Jesus Christ.
Among many other things, this means that Jesus
knows what it means to have to live life day in and
day out. He knows what it is to be bitterly disap-
pointed, to be hurt, and to be rejected. Jesus knows
what it is to love and be loved. He understands the
weariness and anxiety that comes with responsibility.
Jesus is no stranger to death.

Jesus knows us, understands us, and wants to be
our constant companion in all of the circumstances
of life. We do not have to face a single day of our
lives alone. Jesus knows us, and for that we can offer
thanks. Perhaps this prayer will help you express

your gratitude for the presence of an understanding
Christ in your life.

> Lord, I marvel
> that you became a person.
> You have . . .
> walked the earth that I walk;
> breathed the air that I breathe;
> tasted the water that I taste.
> You have . . .
> hurt as I hurt;
> been joyful as I am joyful;
> loved as I love.
> Lord, I thank you from my heart
> for loving me enough
> to experience life as I experience it.
> Accept . . .
> my gratitude,
> my loyalty,
> my love.
> Amen.

Work Out Your Salvation
2:12-13

*Therefore, my beloved, as you have always
obeyed, so now, not only as in my presence but much
more in my absence, work out your own salvation
with fear and trembling; for God is at work in you,
both to will and to work for his good pleasure
(2:12-13, RSV).*

The scene is a campground. Darkness is falling,
and the red flames twist and arch as they eat at a

stack of logs. The campers sit staring into the fire. It is peaceful, and one can feel the presence of God.

A girl speaks from somewhere in the back of the group. As she speaks, a tale of failure unfolds. She recounts her lack of success in school, family, friendships, and love. Bringing her story to a close, she says, "Things have been rough for me. But I do not let them bother me. I just leave all my worries to God."

From somewhere in the group a young man says, "Amen!"

STOP!

Before we "amen" this sort of statement, we need a bit more information. Just exactly what does this girl mean when she says that she leaves all her worries to God?

If she means that she talks with God about her failures, accepts his forgiveness, and goes back to wrestle with her problems, then we can certainly say "amen." But if she means that she dumps her problems on God and waits for him to solve those problems without any help from her—well, that's a different matter!

In my own Christian pilgrimage, I have found that God expects me to work hard at solving my problems. Sure, God has given me forgiveness for my sins; but he has insisted that I be a full partner in the shaping of my life. It works something like this. God has given me truths in the Bible for daily living, and he has given me enough intelligence to understand many of those truths. But my responsibility is to try and apply Bible truths to my daily relationships with other people. My responsibility is to try and make use of what the Bible teaches as I make decisions each day.

God lets me be free to make the best possible decision that I can make in a given situation. Then God works with me to bring the best possible results out of my decision.

We are responsible for what we do with our lives. God accepts the responsibility for helping us become all we can be. If we try and do it all by ourselves, we sin. But if we try to shove all the responsibility for our lives off on God, we also sin.

Over the last few years, this has proven to be a helpful prayer for me in moments of decision.

> Father, I thank you for giving me
> the freedom to make up my mind.
> Help me now; be a partner to me
> as I try to make this decision.
> Grant me insight that I might
> make a wise choice.
> Grant me strength that I might
> bear the consequences of my choice.
> Help me, Lord, to work out my
> salvation with fear and trembling.
>   Amen.

Try and think of some areas in your life that need attention. Begin to pray about these things and try to make the best decision you can about them. Ask God to help you work out the implications of your decisions in your daily life.

Right Priorities

3:7

But all those things that I might count as profit I now reckon as loss, for Christ's sake (3:7, GNB).

This is just the way she told it to me:

"Well, I wasn't making any headlines, but I wasn't doing badly, either. I was busy about my life, doing all the stuff I was supposed to do. I had a good job, a list of past achievements that made my resumé look pretty good, and a good reputation. Popular, content, active. When I went to bed at night, I felt good about the day. I wasn't always sure just what it was that I'd done that day—a lot of stuff I did was busy-work—but I knew I'd been working at it.

"That was the keynote to my life. . . . I was busy working at it. Then I found out I had leukemia. Suddenly, all the stuff I'd been doing paled. It was all so insignificant. I had been working at my life instead of living it.

"Now, because life is precious to me, and because I know what it means not to have the prospect of endless summers, I am living. Really living for the first time. Spending more time with my family and friends than I do with work. Not that I don't work anymore. I still work. And probably more effectively than I did before because I haven't got the time anymore for nonessentials. Before I lived for work. Now, work enables me to live. There's a difference. Now I know what's important, what's worth staking your life on—because that's exactly what I'm doing."

Rather clumsily, I asked, "How long have you got?"

"The rest of my life," she replied. "I will live the rest of my life, and I will die only after my life is over."

Often we hear of events that "put things into perspective" for people. Close calls with death, the death of a friend or loved one, sickness (terminal or curable), injury—all these happenings can cause us to look up for a moment from the race of life to reevaluate what's real and important. And people who take the time, or who are stirred, to take a good hard look at their lives, usually change some things. For things once considered ultimate tend to fade in other contexts.

Paul reexamined his life. But the event that prodded him into a new look at his life was his encounter with Jesus Christ. In the light of day, that is, the truth of God's Son, all else seems to fade. Indeed, it does fade. Always. God's truth makes us act differently than we would act if we'd never heard.

> The lion has roared;
> who will not fear?
> The Lord God has spoken;
> who can but prophesy?
> (Amos 3:8, RSV)

God spoke to Paul, even as he speaks to us—through Jesus. How can we not bear witness to that in our lives?

One day Jesus had been talking to a group who followed him. But they didn't like his words, so they all left, all except the twelve. Turning to them Jesus asked, "And you—would you like to leave also?" Peter said, "Where would we go? We believe you are the Holy One from God" (John 6:67-69, author's paraphrase). Peter couldn't go back to mere fishing after he'd seen the Christ. He couldn't follow anyone else—he'd been with Jesus. Nothing in life measured up to his experience of Christ.

And so it was with Paul. All was loss in the light of Christ. And so it should be with us. Our priorities should reflect our encounter with Christ. The way we live our lives tells to the world how well we have heard the voice of God. Our lives show whether we've really experienced Christ or not.

Father, Creator of all life,
Help me live the life you've given to me for all
    of my life,
So that I may show that I have, indeed, encoun-
    tered, and been encountered by you on the way.

                     In Christ's name,
                     Amen.

The Gift of Righteousness
3:9

*I no longer have a righteousness of my own, the
kind that is gained by obeying the Law. I now have
the righteousness that is given through faith in
Christ, the righteousness that comes from God and is
based on faith (3:9, GNB).*

I don't remember everything the preacher said. In
fact, there's really only one word that keeps coming
back to me, and that word is *wilderness*. He said
something about how funny Mark's first few verses
would have sounded to a good Jew in Jesus' time.
The good news of God beginning in the wilderness?
Why, everyone knew that God's words for men were
found at the Temple.

But, the preacher said, the *wilderness* was where
the gospel of Jesus began, just as it is in *our* wilderness that the gospel always begins.

And he had me. Because I know my life is mostly
wilderness. I try to clothe that wilderness in the illu-
sions of comfort, security, happiness, joy. But when
all the nonessentials are stripped away, when I stand

before God naked, alone, and honest, I know my life is dry, wasted, arid—a wilderness. I'm a sinner, a hopeless sinner.

I go to church because of what I don't feel—the presence of God—as much as I go because of what I do feel. I go wanting to hear that there is hope, that there is salvation, that there is joy. I go not wanting to hear any of those things because I know that if I do hear it, the feeble balance will be upset. The thin foundation of security upon which I have built my existence, that curious mixture of ignored hopelessness, denied loneliness, shunned pain, all that will crumble.

And it did. The balance was tipped. The foundation crumbled. My castle was washed away in the tide of God's Word. Once more, I was in the wilderness. And the truth the preacher forced me to wear the yoke of my own unrighteousness. The chafing of wilderness heat on my neck hurts far worse than the plastic face I normally wear.

Oh God, what shall I do. I hurt so. All my days are spent in tricking, self-deception—tricking myself into thinking that I am good, happy, content.

Yet the truth of the matter is that I live in a desert—barren of life.

The barrenness dries me up continually. On my own, I am dry and getting drier. Hopeless. Helpless. Nothing to count for goodness' sake—and nobody knows it better than I do.

I live in the wilderness. My life is wilderness.

What shall I do?

And somehow I heard him say:

"Why didn't you listen to the man? You lost him after he went to the desert. But that's not the end of my word. My word always starts where it's empty and barren, for that's where my word is needed most. The beginning of the good news is in the wilderness. The continuation of the good news is how I give unto them that need, how I impart to those without, how I count as righteous those who are not.

"You prayed that no one knows your sin better than yourself. Well, I do. I know better than you to what degree you're unrighteous because I know what true righteousness is and you don't. But the gospel of my Son is good news for you—that even though you are sinful, unrighteous, without hope, I love you. And that counts for more than obeying the Law.

"If you will trust me, trust that I love you, accept that I accept you, I will impart new hope, new joy, new righteousness to you. Without me, you will always feel the wind of the wilderness and that wind will always blow your house away. But through faith and trust in me, you will have new clothes of right-eousness. And your wilderness will be futile—no more false faces, no more pretense, no more shaky foundations. Just honesty, truth, and righteousness as the cornerstone of your life."

Good News. For me. And for all who will hear.

The Transforming Christ
3:21

He will change our weak mortal bodies and make them like his own glorious body, using that power by which he is able to bring all things under his rule (3:21, GNB).

There once was a basketball team, lowly and weak. I mean these poor boys were pitiful. Their coach must have mused, "Well, we're not big or fast—but we can't shoot, either." Their arch-rival, meanwhile, had a team composed of fast boys who could definitely shoot—and were they ever big. Giants, every one—or so it seemed.

As the day for the annual contest between the two teams approached, the outlook for the small team was bleak. To make matters worse, this small team would help to celebrate their school's homecoming—apparently by offering themselves as a sacrifice to the other team's giants.

The first half of the contest went about as expected. The teams were mismatched. The big guys played cat-and-mouse with the small guys, making sport of the situation.

Meanwhile, unbeknown to the participants, a chemistry professor at the small school had been working on a mysterious substance which seemed to defy the laws of gravity. The professor went to the team at the half-time break and put this substance on their tennis shoes.

The second half was a different game altogether. Although still as short and slow as ever, the material on their shoes, called "flubber," allowed the little guys to jump like never before—over and around their taller opponents. They didn't even have to worry about their shooting. With flubber every shot was a lay-up or a dunk! Flubber had transformed a lowly and weak bunch of ballplayers into a great team!

Those who are Walt Disney fans will remember the preceeding to be the story line of "The Absent-Minded Professor." The movie is a classic of comic fantasy.

Yet many people will read Philippians 3:17-19, as well as other verses like 4:13 and believe that Christ's transforming power for us is kind of like putting spiritual flubber onto our tennis shoes. We are then able to behave and respond to situations beyond our human abilities, jumping over problems, making every basket in life's game. Christ somehow makes us a winner over every obstacle which stands in our way.

Can this be what Paul meant? He had been beaten, scourged, spat upon, exiled, ridiculed, and laughed at. Paul had a lot of problems in which some spiritual flubber would have come in handy. No. Paul speaks of the final transformation of our bodies and lives. And it's transformation—not addition.

This transformation by Christ will come when Jesus comes from heaven to receive us unto himself. Our inward nature will be made to correspond to the nature of Christ. The word for "to be like" (RSV) or "make them like" (GNB) (*summorphos*) carries the notion of "character." Then our outward bodies will be transformed to correspond to our inner transformation (*metachamatisei*, "will change"). Our transformation will then be complete—inward, as well as outward, transformation.

That's all well and good, but what of now? How is this passage applicable to us now?

One thing's for sure. Our bodies are not transformed outwardly yet. Arthritis, knee injuries, sickness, and fatigue still plague us. We will have to wait until Jesus comes back for *that* transformation to take place. We'll have to wait until then for the total transformation of which Paul here speaks.

But even as we have encountered the Christ and have been saved by God's love through him, we begin to experience a transformation of our inner-selves. Paul calls it "having the mind of Christ." The power of God in us allows us to see things from a more Christlike perspective. We are able to take advantage of the presence of the Spirit in our thought and decision-making processes.

So our transformation is now, but not yet; just as our salvation is present, but not complete. Even as our salvation will be fulfilled only in the presence of God in heaven, so will our transformation only be completed at that time. Yet, we can begin to experience what that will be like. We experience transformation now and use what we experience. But we look forward to that day of consummation as well.

Father,
Continue transforming us, even as we wait to be
    totally transformed.
As we look to the day when we shall be no longer
    limited by the weakness of our mortality,
Help us to know that the power of Christ, even
    now, enables us to rise above much of the pet-
    tiness of life, to meet the real issues head-on.
Not overpowered by the world, but empowered by
    your salvation to us
Help us learn to live transformed lives, even as we
    are continually being transformed.
                    In the name of Christ Jesus,
                    Amen.

II
Discipleship

Servants

1:1; 2:4

Paul and Timothy, servants of Christ Jesus . . . .
Let each of you look not only to his own interests,
but also to the interests of others (1:1; 2:4, RSV).

The story has been told about the man who, with
tears in his eyes, went to talk to his best friend. "My
life is ruined. I just learned that my business partner
embezzled everything we own and ran off with the
money."

"That's bad," his friend answered, "but look at
the bright side—it could be worse."

"But there's more," the man continued. "Last
night my only son called and told my wife and me
he's dropping out of college and that we would never
see him again."

"That is bad," the friend returned, "but *still*,
everything considered, it could be worse."

"Hold it a second," exploded the man. "I've told
you all my problems, and terribly big ones at that,
and all you keep saying is, 'It could be worse.' "

"Why man," the friend exclaimed, "it could be
worse, in fact, it could be much worse. Everything
that has happened to you could have happened to
me."

We really do live in a world where people are primarily concerned with themselves. Each one of us
seems to act out of his own best interest. In today's
society, a move is not made unless it is considered
profitable or a low-risk endeavor. Most of us make a
practice of watching out for "ole number one."

But what about the message of Christianity? Is it not just the opposite? The life and ministry of Jesus Christ is diametrically opposed to the life-style of the supposed friend mentioned above. Jesus was truly, as Dietrich Bonhoeffer said, "the man for others." Jesus, himself, took "the form of a servant" (2:7). Jesus described his role by saying, "The Son of man came not to be ministered unto, but to minister, and to give his life a ransom for many" (Mark 10:45). Likewise, he charged his followers with the same ministry. Our Lord rejected the world's standards and made the servant role the mark of greatness. He plainly instructed us, "But many that are first shall be last; and the last shall be first" (Matt. 19:30). The greatest title which one may receive is not "master" or "father" or "teacher"; it is "servant" (Matt. 23:6-11). The twelve were sent out with the commission to preach that the kingdom of heaven had drawn nigh, to heal the sick, to raise the dead, to cleanse the lepers, to cast out demons, and to give freely even as they had received freely.

In short, we are to give of ourselves, following in Jesus' steps. That means we are called upon to live in a way radically different from the life-style of the world. We must embody God's concerns and extend ourselves to all who are in need. That is servanthood. It is truly a bold mission.

Father,
It is so hard to see beyond myself,
but this day let me look to Jesus Christ
    who came as a lowly servant.
Let me remember that he came—
—not to be ministered to, but to minister,
—not to seek his own gain, but to give to others,
—not as a powerful king, but as a lowly servant.

I want to be like him, Father.
I pledge my life, as your servant, like he did.

Amen.

Saints
1:2

To all the saints in Christ Jesus at Philippi, together with the overseers and deacons (1:2, NIV).

"Father, my heart goes out to you this day, for I feel so small and unworthy. I think of those that have gone before me—

Abraham, who was willing even to offer his son;
Moses, the lawgiver, who stretched forth his rod
    and the waters were parted;
Samson, the mighty one;
Elijah, who stood alone against Baal;
David, the great king;
Solomon, and all his wisdom;
Isaiah, the great prophet;
Amos, the preacher;
Hosea, who knew of true love;
John the Baptist, the forerunner;
Peter, James, and John, the closest of the
    disciples;
Paul, who saw Jesus on the Damascus Road.

I think of these, my Father, and am overwhelmed. I'm not like them, O God, not like them at all."

Such are the prayers of many of us today. This attitude can possibly be attributed to what we might call a "big-is-better" syndrome. We often fool ourselves by saying or believing that big is better. This is true even in religious circles. The larger churches often are considered as the best or, perhaps, doing the work of the Lord better than anyone else. And where is the small church or the average Christian? I guess we simply aren't important.

To be small in America usually denotes inadequacy, insufficiency, immaturity—a loser. Small churches are frequently seen, and see themselves, as organizations that failed to grow as expected or as a church that has gone downhill or as an isolated group that never got the message that bigger is better. Thus this message is passed on to individuals, and they are convinced that since they haven't done big things they aren't important.

But a striking message is found here in Paul's opening words. He addressed this letter to the "saints" in Philippi. This word means "holy ones," and it places these Christians of the small town of Philippi on the same level as every saint that has ever lived. Jesus speaks of this same truth in the parable of the mustard seed (Matt. 13:31-32). He points to the worth and value of the "smallest of seeds," which grows into a great tree, providing shelter for the birds of the air. It is like a single match which can dispel the darkness of any closed-off room. It is like the small source of light in a car headlight which sends forth a great cone of light. It is like the tremendous difference a few grains of salt can make. Jesus, himself, bears witness to this truth. Whoever would have thought that a babe from a manger could save the world? Jesus spoke often of the significance of the little—the grain of mustard seed, the one talent, the cup of cold water, the widow's mite, the lost coin, and even the kindness done unto "one of the least of these."

This is to say, regardless of our stature or accomplishment we should and can feel significant. Although the world stands against us, we know that we are not called upon, necessarily, to do the big things. It is quite possible to be of the greatest use by doing what looks like little things. By being of service in the ordinary everyday things we, in the end, serve God. We are saints of the one true God. We are saints with Paul and all the rest.

Memories
1:3

I thank my God for you every time I remember you (1:3, GNB).

I can see her still. Extremely thin, and a little stooped by age, she looked even smaller from the car than she really was. Her face was wrinkled but eternally youthful with love and life. And her eyes were bright, full of wit and wisdom, clear and sharp. The glasses were unnecessary, I was convinced. Like all grandmothers, she could see everything, just like she knew everything—before I had a chance to tell her.

And there she stood on her doorstep waving good-bye to her youngest son and her favorite grandchildren (or if we weren't the favorites, we could never tell because she always made such a fuss over us). We could tell from the road she was crying as she waved good-bye. Sorry to see us go. Missing us already.

And we'd miss her. We'd miss her big breakfasts with thick-sliced bacon and milk gravy and playing around the massive pine and cedar trees in her big backyard. We'd miss her stories about where our family had been and where we were going.

All that was years ago. But I can remember. Remember her, and what she meant to me.

It's kind of funny though. I have to really work hard to remember the breakfasts, the trees, or the stories. I remember the good-byes the best. I remember her tears as she stood on the porch, lifting her feeble old hand to wave. I remember our tears as we said good-bye for the last time.

Those memories make me sad.

But if I take the time to get past the good-byes to the breakfasts and the trees and the stories, then I'm happy again. I'm a little boy again, clinging to her housecoat. Her absence now is replaced by her new presence in my memory. I'm able to remember how much I loved her, how much I still love her, and how much she meant to me. I'm able to remember all of that, and she lives again, when I take time to remember.

Paul took time to remember his friends. I'm sure that some of those memories were sad. He'd said good-bye, he missed them; he longed, perhaps futilely, to see them again. He remembered times together with them which he'd never know again—melancholy memories.

But then he remembered more. He could see himself in Philippi talking with the other believers there. He remembered the bond of love which could never separate them. He remembered their common faith, their common joy, their common hope. And through his memories, he was strengthened anew. The memories of yesterday encouraged him for the present and gave him hope for the future.

Because Paul remembered, he thanked God. He thanked God for the blessings of good friends who were significant even when they were apart. Memories let people live for us again.

There are many people, though, who don't like to remember. They've never worked through the grief of the good-byes or the hurt is still too sharp.

But memory is a gift God gives us. It is a gift which allows important people in our lives to stay with us, to affect us, to encourage us. Our memory allows us to see where we've been, so that we may start again where we're going. And more than anything, memory allows us to see where in our lives God has been—in people, places, events—so that we may know where to look for him in every new today.

> Father,
> Thank you for the gift of memory
> Help us remember
>   important people
>   important places
>   important events
> and the lessons they have taught us.
> When the memory hurts, comfort us
> So that we may let our past inform our
>   every present.
> Through the Lord of Past, Present, and Future—
> Amen.

In Every Prayer
1:4

Always in every prayer of mine for you all making my prayer with joy (1:4, RSV).

Eternal God, in whom all that is made is made; unto you I lift up my soul, for you have been the hope and joy of all generations, and in every age you have given men and women the power to seek you and in seeking to find you. At this time, O God, do not allow me to pray as I so often pray—

Let not any room of my heart be closed to you;

Let not my will be contrary to yours,

Let not resentment toward others remain,

Let me not return to idle thoughts and idle ways.

But in this prayer, yes, "in every prayer"—

Let me praise your glorious name. My soul boasts in you. Almighty God, you are from eternity to eternity, you spoke and the light pushed the darkness away, you made all things good. O God you are strong, wise, holy, full of tender mercy; you made me in your own image. I praise you and bless your holy name.

And in this prayer, yes, "in every prayer"—

Let me offer thanksgivings unto you. I thank you, you who are immortal, for lending a listening ear to the prayers of mortal men. I lift up my heart in gratitude:

For happiness,

For the mere joy of living,

For this good earth,

For friends and relatives,

For churches and homes,

but most supremely, I give you thanks for your fatherly love as revealed in your only Son Jesus Christ my Lord.

And in this prayer, yes, "in every prayer"—

Let me confess of things unpure, for I know you are faithful and just. I must confess:

I am negligent concerning the spiritual;

—quick to play, slow to pray,

—willing to receive, unwilling to give,

—desire the good, but do the evil,

—eager to condemn, reluctant to forgive.

I grieve and lament before you, and I cry out to

you with the words of the apostle Paul, "Wretched man that I am! Who will deliver me from this body of death? Thanks be to God through Jesus Christ our Lord!"

And in this prayer, yes, "in every prayer"—

May I raise up petitions and intercessions before you.

Grant me—
> the gift to be charitable,
> the grace of understanding,
> the joy of your salvation.

Now to others my attention turns—
> for all who stand for truth,
> for all who are working for peace,
> for all who suffer for righteousness' sake.

As in this prayer, Father, so "in every prayer," may I remember to praise you and thank you. May I be willing to confess my known sin; and let me not forget, while offering my petitions, to intercede on the behalf of others.

> As in every prayer,
> Amen.

I Long for You All

1:8

For God is my witness, how I yearn for you all with the affection of Christ Jesus (1:8, RSV).

O God, our Maker, Defender, Redeemer, and Friend; you who are the Father of all humankind. You have demonstrated your love for us by sending Jesus Christ our Lord, and have enriched our human life by the radiance of his presence. Praise and thanks be unto you for this your Greatest Gift.

For his light in the midst of my darkness,

For his direction in the midst of my waywardness.

For his belief in the midst of my unbelief.

For his obedience in the midst of my disobedience.

For his love in the midst of my unloveliness.

And perhaps today, my Father, for this I am most grateful—

His love, his unending love;

For the record of his deeds of love,

I give you thanks.

Grant that the remembrance of these deeds, yes, his very life which was lived on this very earth under these same skies, would awake me to a life of love.

That I could "yearn" for others

with the affection of Christ.

Hear me, O God, and know my struggles. It is hard for me to love when I'm not loved in return. I now kneel before you in lowly adoration with these words of confession—

I know not how to love.

You, who are Love, must love through me.

O most loving God, who in Jesus Christ did make known your love to me and even now continue doing the same in and through me, I ask of you this one thing—as I pray in the stillness of this moment—

That I could "yearn" for others

with the affection of Christ.

For there are those that are heavy on my heart—

All who are without the love of a family,

All who cannot sleep because of despair,

All who suffer pain,

All who are facing danger,

All who are hungry and cold,

Give to them all the calm assurance of your presence,

yes, even may the hungry be fed, may the hated be loved, may the distraught be lifted by men and women who are captured by your love. I feel for them every one; my thoughts go out to them today. Grant your blessing also, I pray, to all on this globe who serve in Christ's name,

All ministers of the gospel,
All social workers,
All doctors and nurses,
All who know how to give,
All who love.

May your great purposes be accomplished through each one. Grant them the awareness of your presence.

And, now, for me—that I could "yearn" for others with the affection of Christ. That I might love as you have loved me. In Jesus' name,

Amen.

Death . . . Life
1:20

As it is my eager expectation and hope that I shall not be at all ashamed, but that with full courage now as always Christ will be honored in my body, whether by life or death (1:20, RSV).

A father sat calmly one Saturday morning watching his busy-as-a-beaver son scurry around the yard at a frenzied pace. Suddenly the child burst into the garage and exclaimed, "Where on earth does the time go?"

"Why, son," the father replied, "the things you do eat it all up." Such is life.

A funny thing happened to me on the way through school. As a student in elementary school, I longed to be in high school. I dreamed of one day wearing a class ring. But when I got the ring, it looked small compared to a college ring. So my life turned toward the future of my college days. Things would be great then. I couldn't wait! Well, my college days came and the same thing happened again—my thoughts kept looking forward to the days ahead in seminary. There is no telling how much thought and energy was wasted, always living in the future, anticipating something else, never really able to live in the present. Where does time go? It goes into everything we do—our work, play, sleep, eating, worship, daydreams, yearnings, idleness, service, misbehavior, moods—our lives, and the events that make up our lives, eat time up.

Have you ever played the game "what if?" Sure, we all have. Well, "what if" our physical life here on this planet would never come to an end? That would solve the problem of time that we all have. We'd have plenty of time and could get so much accomplished, or would we? We are all such terrible procrastinators as it is. Can you imagine how long it would be before some of us got around to educating ourselves or securing a job if we thought we would never die? Would we ever cease playing or would we rather continue postponing things indefinitely?

Often when a person has had a heart attack, learned he has cancer, been in an accident, come close to drowning, or been close to some other kind of peril, he will make promises about how he is going to live with more awareness of time, a deeper commitment to God, and greater concern for others. Sometimes we mean these words, but most of us forget our good intentions. The fact is—death does slap us awake to the limitations of time which are imposed on each of us.

Instead of shattering all meaning from life, death, in a very real sense, is that which makes us live. It compels us to see the significance of life. The very fact that we know that we will not live here forever, should force us to confront the question: What am I doing with the life I have?

At a particular point in Jesus' life, the Bible says that he "set his face to go to Jerusalem" (Luke 9:51). At that time Jesus affirmed the inevitability of death for him. As it has been said, he walked beneath the shadow of the cross. When we learn to live with an awareness of our death, we will be on the right path toward worthy living. Life will take on deeper meaning.

We fool ourselves if we believe "length of days" is the mark of a significant life. Methuselah lived to be 969 years old, but the only noteworthy thing about his life is a list of his children. On the other hand, Jesus was only 33 years old when he died. His accomplishment is judged not by the length of his life, but the quality of it.

So in order to live a life "worthy of the gospel of Christ" (1:27, RSV), we must concern ourselves with the limitation of time and how to best use it. Our selection of priorities, what we consider important, will determine how we spend our time. Simply spoken, if you knew you were going to die at the end of this year, what would your priorities be? What would you seek to do in the remaining time? What would claim your attention? We must ask ourselves this question because death is not a "what if" game. Death is sure.

In answer to this question, admittedly we all would seek, for one thing, to participate in the beauty of nature. We would make the most of all five senses, glorying in all the facets of the wonder of this good earth. Secondly, our relationships with others—family, church, work, school—would become very important. Some relationships we would wish to build, while others would need mending. Thirdly, and supremely, each one of us would not dare allow these final days pass without examining and reaffirming our relationship with God. Like the criminal who hung on the third cross, we would turn our eyes to Jesus, he who is life.

Father,

Since death is certain, may this certainty force me to live—

> with greater awareness of time,
> with greater appreciation of nature,
> with greater concern for others,
> with greater love for you.

Amen.

Doing What's Necessary
1:21-24

For what is life? To me, it is Christ. Death, then, will bring more. But if by continuing to live I can do more worthwhile work, then I am not sure which I should choose. I am pulled in two directions. I want very much to leave this life and be with Christ, which is a far better thing (1:21-23, GNB).

If you had a picture of him, you could see it in his eyes. And you could recognize the look—kind of sad, or wistful, or far away, like he was catching a glimpse of a whole other world, a world where he belonged.

If you had a picture of him, and the picture had a caption, it might have said something like, "I'm glad to be here . . . but I'd rather be somewhere else." And you'd know he meant no insult, no discourtesy. He'd be there, and he'd be glad to be there. But deep down, underneath the "glad," you'd know he really would rather be somewhere else.

Who do we speak of here? Paul? Of course. But not Paul alone. We speak of all those servants of God who somehow put the work of the kingdom on a higher priority than their personal comfort or satisfaction.

—the lady schoolteacher, who sees her vocation as part of her work as for God, who faces the cold of February's winter for the sake of those young minds, when she'd really rather stay at home in the warmth.

—the preacher who spends his evenings visiting, meeting, studying, and does it out of commitment—but he'd love to spend some time with his family, really spend time with them.

—the doctor, who goes to the hospital to care for those who need help, and who wistfully thinks that he doesn't remember what his easy chair feels like.

And there's the story of Paul. Paul the servant, the old saint, who longed to go home to be with God, who longed to see clearly, to understand, and to know. Paul was the embattled messenger of Christ who, deep in his soul, just wanted to rest, to be with Christ, and to experience the comfort heaven would give. Heaven had been his goal for a lifetime; and now he felt he was getting close to reaching his goal. He wanted to reach it.

Yet, there was another call besides the inner call to heaven. That other call was duty and responsibility to those who looked to him for strength and guidance.

There were new Christians who needed upbuilding and strengthening in the faith. For while he wanted to be in heaven with Christ, Paul was for others like a "dose of heaven," a real representation of the Lord; he was needed on earth. Personally, he would have liked to rest. But for the sake of the gospel—always he acted thus—he felt he must remain to work for those who needed him.

How well do we reflect what Paul lived? And did not Paul live in imitation of the life of Jesus, who was the most unselfish? For Jesus it was, "Not my will, but thine." For Paul it was, "I long to go home, but there is work yet to do."

Jesus and Paul both had personal interests in what they did. Yet they did not let their personal concerns control their actions. Jesus loves us more than his own life. Paul loved his friends too much to allow himself the luxury of resting. Rather, the will of God and the good they could do for others, through that will, was the dominant factor in their lives.

May we pray for that kind of motivation.

Father,

I sometimes can't get up for church on Sunday,

And I rarely go out of my way for others—unless
somehow it is really for me through them that
I go out of my way.

And I am always more concerned with my comfort
than with your will.

Forgive me. And in forgiving me, grant me
strength to see anew the needs of those
around me, the needs that make taking
it easy a blasphemous way of life.

Rather, help me see that in Christ I have duty
and responsibility to your children,

Help me do what needs to be done.

Help me do your will, even if I have to go out
of my way to do it.
Even as your Son went out of his way for us—
Amen.

Worthy Living
1:27

Only let your manner of life be worthy of the gospel of Christ (1:27, RSV).

A little boy was standing with his father on a railroad platform when a shiny new locomotive churned into the station. The excited boy at once edged up to the engine. "Daddy," he started, "please ask the driver how much this engine cost." The good-natured driver, overhearing the boy's request, supplied the answer by naming a substantial sum of money.

"My," remarked the father, "our new church cost about the same!"

The words were hardly out of his mouth when the boy, pointing at the engine, innocently said, "Yes, Daddy, but *this* works!"

It doesn't take one long to realize that the attitude toward Christianity by the average person outside the church is much the same as this little boy. It is tragic that so often this attitude is not without justification: Christianity rightly related to one's everyday manner of life is hard to find in much of organized religion today.

The trouble is that many professed Christians study, even preach the good news of Christianity, but do not live it. The teachings of Jesus never seem to penetrate daily living. Oh sure, we live it most on Sunday's, but what about Monday through Saturday? Is Christianity evident in our homelife, at school, at work, and at play? An old philosopher was convinced that the teachings of other great men were only worth their weight if they were put into practice. Nothing else would satisfy him but to practice what he taught. He often asked his students, "What has your reading done for you?" Then, quite matter of factly, he would add, "If you don't intend to live like a philosopher, then don't come back!"

Those words sound strikingly similar, do they not, to the words of Jesus. "Not every one who says to me, 'Lord, Lord,' shall enter the kingdom of heaven, but he who does the will of my Father who is in heaven" (Matt. 7:21, RSV). We might well humble ourselves to learn an important lesson from the old philosopher and be careful not to consider ourselves Christians until we can show convincingly that Christianity does work in everyday life, just like the locomotive.

Paul said, "Let your manner of life be worthy of the gospel of Christ" (1:27, RSV). This is impossible if the gospel does not become a part of our daily walk. To be worthy of the gospel is an impossibility in itself. But, according to Paul, Christ lives in through us, equipping us for this high calling. Thus, Christ's life and ministry is a model to us. His desires are to become our desires; his goals, our goals; his concerns, our concerns. Here is the key to worthy living—it is coming to grips with the desires, goals, and concerns of Jesus Christ—as it is written: "The Spirit of the Lord is upon me, because he has anointed me to preach good news to the poor. He has sent me to proclaim release to the captives and recovering of sight to the blind, to set at liberty those who are oppressed, to proclaim the acceptable year of the Lord" (Luke 4:18-19, RSV). Simply stated, Jesus' life was worthy because his concerns were directed toward others. May our lives become one with his as we do for others what he has done for us.

Servanthood
2:5-7

Have this attitude in yourselves which was also in Christ Jesus, who, although He existed in the form of God, did not regard equality with God a thing to be grasped, but emptied Himself, taking the form of a bond-servant, and being made in the likeness of men (2:5-7, NASB).

A disciple is not above his teacher, nor a slave above his master. It is enough for the disciple that he become as his teacher, and the slave as his master (Matt. 10:24-25, NASB).

Lord, when I first became a Christian, I wanted to be just like Jesus. I wanted to walk the road of life that he had walked, think the thoughts that had occupied his mind, and feel the emotions that had surged through his heart. I wanted to be to other people what Jesus had been during his earthly life: a friend, a counselor, a pillar of strength amid the weakening storms of life.

Now I am not so sure.

I am not sure, Lord, that I actually desire to be like Jesus. For now I begin to see the truth about Jesus, and that truth is frightening. Scared and trembling, I find that I must admit a terrible thing.

Jesus Christ was a slave.

Jesus Christ was a slave to your will, Lord. For the sake of obedience, he left his place of perfect safety and absolute power, entered this dangerous and sinful world, and was killed by those he came to help. That is all well and good for Jesus, Lord; but I am not so sure that it is for me.

You see, Lord, I have always wanted to play the role of your child. There is something wonderful, peaceful, and reassuring about thinking of myself as a child of God. I suppose that this is the case because of the shape of my childhood. As a child, I was never expected to do anything dangerous—in fact, I was discouraged from attempting such activities. As a child, I was often taught how to win, but I was generally spared the pain of learning what it felt like to lose. As a child, I seldom had to bear a great deal of responsibility for anything; I could always rely on my family to take care of me. Most of all, Lord, when I was a child, I was allowed to ignore the reality of the world's pain. In fact, I was most often shielded from pain. Given all of this, I think you can understand why I have always wanted to be your child, Lord. And when I first heard that Jesus Christ was your Son, I thought that I would become your child by following him.

And I was right. The trouble is that I misunderstood what it meant to be your child. To be your child, I must become your servant, your slave. That scares me, Lord; for as your servant I am subject to your demands. You can require that I enter into a losing situation in order to bring your presence and power to people. If I become your servant, I will be required not only to recognize the pain that is in the world but also to become a part of the life of those who suffer. God, you can insist that I take the hurts and sufferings of other people into my own heart, that I carry their burdens upon my shoulders. Lord, if I become your servant, you may require me to do these things even if those for whom I labor turn upon me and kill me.

Lord, I am not sure that I want anything to do with this servanthood business. Can't I just be your child?

"Little one, I am sorry, but you are not my child if you are not my servant. I am either God to you, Lord of all that is you, or I am not your Father.

"But you do not understand clearly what it means to be my servant. When you are my servant, I do not make you do anything. I will not force you to endure pain, threaten you until you minister to others, or order you into a combat you cannot win. For I am God, and that way is not my way.

"When you become my child and my servant, you will find that you are filled with a desire to discover my will for all things. Above all else, you will begin to love me. And as the years of your life pass, you will learn to love all of the world and each part of the world as I love. It is this love that will drive you, that will impel you, to open wide your heart to the pain of those around you. This love will inspire you to pray for those who love you, those who hate you, and even those who do not know that you exist. This love, the love that led Jesus to assume the likeness of men, will lead you to offer your life for the sake of others' lives. You will lose yourself in my sea of love and, in so losing yourself, discover the world, yourself, and me."

Dear Lord and Father:
We confess that we have often played
at being your children and servants.
Forgive us of our folly and fear.
We come before you asking

that you might fill our hearts
with love for you.
We ask that you help us to love
even as you love.
And we ask that we may be driven by love
from our comfortable, safe places of rest
into the dangerous places of need
that fill the world.
For we would be your children and servants,
even as Jesus was your child and servant.
In the name of him who humbled himself,
taking the form of a bondservant.

                                        Amen.

Bowing My Knees
2:9-11

Therefore God has highly exalted him and bestowed on him the name which is above every name, that at the name of Jesus every knee should bow, in heaven and on earth and under the earth, and every tongue confess that Jesus Christ is Lord, to the glory of God the Father (2: 9-11, RSV).

Father, I think that I want to bow down before Christ and worship. I am nearly certain that I want to confess Jesus Christ as Lord of creation and Lord of my life. But there is this problem, Father. I am a little embarrassed about it, but I will tell you about it anyway.

You see, Lord, my knees do not bend so well, Now please do not mistake me. My knees are fine for most things—running, jumping, swimming, holding children. But I do not normally bow down and confess anyone to be my master. I am afraid that I do not know how to do that sort of thing. Can you help me, Lord?

"Little one, the problem is not that you do not know how to bow down and worship. Why, your knees have been bowed in worship during most of your life—although you did not realize it.

"You have worshiped many things in your lifetime. I have seen you bow down before the power of the crowd. I have been watching, and I have seen your devotion to status. And I have even beheld you as you worshiped yourself, confessing yourself and your desires to be the lord of your life.

"Little one, you are really very good at worshiping things. Your knees are very pliable, and they bend and bow easily. But you have problems when it comes to knowing what is worthy of worship.

"Still, if you are willing to learn, I can help you."

Father, I will be your student. Under your watchful eye, I will learn to know what is worthy of worship. With my hand in yours, I will bow down before Jesus and confess with my tongue that he is Lord.

Make a list of the things that strongly influence you as you make decisions. Are you worshiping these things rather than God? Pray and ask God to help you surrender totally to him.

Lights to the World
2:14-16

Do all things without grumbling or questioning, that you may be blameless and innocent, children of God without blemish in the midst of a crooked and

*perverse generation, among whom you shine as lights
in the world, holding fast the word of life, so that in
the day of Christ I may be proud that I did not run in
vain or labor in vain." (2: 14-16, RSV).*

It is getting dark out there, Father.

Our sun has set. The dusk is fading, and night is
creeping out from her lair to engulf the world. Death
and disease, poverty and war, hatred and malice—
these giants of the shadow stalk the world, slaying
whom they wish and striking fear in the hearts of all
who see them. The power of darkness, the power of
evil, enslaves the wills of people. They are blind to
their sin, deaf to the pleas of the poor, ignorant of
their own peril. It is getting dark out there, Father,
and I am scared.

In my fright, I want to withdraw from the outside
world. I want to seek shelter from the danger that is
there. But when I flee from the world and withdraw
into myself, I find that the darkness has run ahead of
me. It is there inside of me, quenching the light of my
spirit. Lord, the darkness is there, growing inside of
me! I, like the rest of the world, am mired deeply in
sin. Often, I cannot recognize my own sin; and even
when I do, I cannot always do anything about it. I
am in bondage to darkness, Lord. I stand in the
dungeon of my sin, my limbs in shackles, and I raise
my voice to you: Where is your light? Lord, give me
light!

"My beloved child, you shall have light.

"Because you ask it of me, I shall send the light of
my presence to dwell within your heart. My throne
shall be there, and the darkness shall flee from my
presence. I will break your chains. I will throw open
the doors of your dungeon and bring you forth into
the fresh air of a new day. Together, we will carry a
bright light as we explore all the avenues of your life.

And we shall shine that light on each patch of darkness that we discover, destroying the shadows forever.

"You will become a vessel of light, a crystal filled with a light that can dispel the darkness of the world around you. With the power that is within you, you shall be able to put away fear. Those around you will draw strength from you, and my light shall be kindled in them so that they, too, become lights shining amid the darkness.

"You ask where light may be found. You ask for light with which to illumine your own darkness. I am the light of the world, and I give myself to you so that I might shine through you. Take now this light into your heart and go forth, shining as a beacon of hope in a darkening world."

> Father, in the darkness of these days,
> you have come to us
> as light, as hope.
> Take now our hearts;
> fill them with the searching light
> of your presence.
> Take now our lives;
> mold our lives so that others
> might see you in us.
> Father, make us to be
> lights to the world,
> signposts to your Son.
> We pray in the name of him who said,
> "I am the light of the world."
> > Amen.

Holding Fast the Word of Life
2:16

Holding fast the word of life, so that in the day of Christ I may be proud that I did not run in vain or labor in vain (2:16, RSV).

It had not been one of my outstanding days at school. By the time I got home, after riding the bus for over an hour, I was tired and frustrated. Barging open the door, I stormed into the house and threw my books down in an untidy heap on the couch. Mom looked up from her chair.

"What's the matter with you?" she asked.

"Oh, just the normal things," I said, biting off each word. "Mom, I don't fit in at school. I'm really not interested in who is dating who, in fitting in with the groups, or even in the football team."

"So, what's wrong with that?" came her sensible reply.

"Well, it's not the best way to become popular," I said, stung by her insight.

"Do you want to be popular?" she asked.

"Sure. Doesn't everyone? But it seems as if I can't be a somebody and still be myself."

Mom looked thoughtful for a few moments, then said, "Well, I guess you'll have to decide which is more important—being popular or being yourself. Which would you rather be?"

"I guess I'd rather be myself," I said almost apologetically.

"Then remember that you think that and act that way. I imagine that you will have plenty of friends—people who will like you just for you."

Of course, Mom was right.

Among the most difficult problems in life is to

determine what one thing, above all other things, is most important to us. Some of us take the easy way out and allow other concerns, outside ourselves— society, peer pressure, popularity—to determine our priorities. For instance, we often let ourselves be convinced that money is the single most important part of life. After all, we can look around us and see plenty of people who live as if that were the case. So many people could not be wrong, could they?

Couldn't they?

For better or worse, we are responsible for choosing the focus and priorities of our lives. We may make money or social station or popularity the final criteria for what we do in life. But it is our choice. We may choose family, friends, work, play, church, or self as the point around which to focus our lives, but the choice is our responsibility.

Paul felt that the "Word of life" should be the focal point of his existence. The "Word of life" is the gospel, the good news of Jesus Christ and the living experience of Christ's presence in our lives. Paul was right. What we have heard about Jesus, what we have experienced with Jesus—these are the only adequate focal points for our lives.

Even after we have settled on Jesus Christ as the most important aspect of our lives, we still face the problem of remembering and acting upon that affirmation in the daily rigors of life. There are times of pain, frustration, envy, or embarassment when we are tempted to act like something besides Christians. For example:

—Would you turn down a big promotion with much more money, more prestige, more security for your family if you knew it would involve you in activities of questionable morality?

—Would you really pray for the grace to love someone who had slandered you or a member of your family with malicious gossip?

—Would you give your regular offering to the work of the Lord if you knew that by refusing to do so you could finally buy that extra item you had had your eye on for the last several months?

—Would you surrender part of your free time if you had the opportunity to work with underprivileged children and share your faith?

The challenge is ever before us. Like Paul, our lives should reflect the continued presence of Christ's influence upon us. Our actions, attitudes, and decisions should be made with final reference to the Word of life. We fall short, and so we must confess and repent, even as we pray for God's help as we dedicate ourselves anew to the high calling of Jesus Christ and the examples of Paul.

Oh Lord, Father of our Lord Jesus Christ,
Hear us as we confess that we have often
    lost our way,
    become engrossed in the world's ways,
And forgive us as we repent.
Give us keen eyes
    so that we may see the Son of your love
    and use him as our criteria, our standard,
    our focus of life.
Grant us courage, strength, and wisdom
    that we might hold forth the words of life.
In the name of him, who is himself
    the word of Life.
                Amen.

Plans
2:19

But I hope in the Lord Jesus to send Timothy to you shortly, so that I also may be encouraged when I learn of your condition (2:19, NASB).

It was a hot, steamy day in late June. Out in the fields, the cattle stood quietly in the shade of the trees lining the creek. The family dogs lay beneath the trucks that were parked in the driveway. All was still on my grandparents' farm, resting and seeking to escape from the overpowering heat.

Except me.

Perspiration dripped from my nose, streaking the dust on my face, as I carried long wooden boards from the garage into the backyard. Finishing that task, I rounded up some nails and a hammer and began making about as much racket as a ten-year-old boy can make with that equipment. I was going to build a shed there in the backyard in which to store my things. I had wood, space, nails, and a hammer—nothing could stop me now.

Well, almost nothing.

My grandmother soon came bustling out of the house to find out what all of the noise was about. Sizing up the situation with a glance, she told me that all those boards were probably killing the grass. Furthermore, I would have to get a permit from the county before I could legally build my shed, and that would cost money. With her usual good sense, she convinced me that I might be better off if I would consult with someone before beginning such large projects. She helped me return the wood to the garage, find all the stray nails nestled in the grass, and took me inside the house for a cool drink.

And that, as the saying goes, was that.

We often make plans without consulting God. If we are honest with ourselves, most of us must admit that God has seldom been a factor in our choice of life-style. We have usually decided on our own what would be our career, how to spend our money, where to invest our time—in short, we have made our plans for life and then hoped that God would bless them.

It is easy to imagine that Paul was once the same way. As a young man, he probably dreamed of the day when he would be an adult and a Pharisee. He studied hard, and planned to spend his life interpreting the Law. Perhaps he lay in bed at night imagining what it would be like to be a "Hebrew of Hebrews." When he became a man, Paul achieved his goal. He should have been a happy man. Instead, by his own admission, he was unhappy, frustrated, always trying for perfection but failing and feeling the guilt of his failure.

Could it be that we experience a sense of failure and frustration because we have left God out of our life's plans?

In his later life, Paul realized that all plans should be made with God in mind. He tried to discern the will of God before deciding upon a plan of action; and he realized that all his plans were subject to change. Paul seldom said, "I will do . . . ." Rather, Paul learned to say something like, "I will do this, if the Lord allows."

All of this points to one thing: The only sure thing in life is God. A Christian has taken a giant step forward when he learns to depend upon God's good will toward people. We are to seek and find our security in the fact and experience that God's love remains constant. The best possible plan for our lives is to deliver our lives into the hands of God. After we have done this, it becomes possible to begin mapping out a meaningful Christian plan for the rest of our lives.

Dear Father,
who knows the innermost workings of our hearts:
Forgive us of our excessive pride
that pride which leads us to plan our lives
within the resources of our own strength.
Grant us wisdom,
that we might see and come to trust
in your good will toward us.
Help us bring our lives to you,
that you might shape them
upon the workbench of your will.
We pray this prayer in the name of Jesus Christ,
who placed his trust in you as Father.

                                    Amen.

The Interests of Christ

2:20-21

He is the only one who shares my feelings and who really cares about you. Everyone else is concerned only with his own affairs, not about the cause of Jesus Christ (2:20-21, GNB).

"We're going to look after ourselves from now on and touch our caps to nobody. See?"

That's right," said the other Dwarfs. "We're on our own now, No more Aslan, no more kings, no more silly stories about other worlds. The Dwarfs are for the Dwarfs."[1]

In C. S. Lewis' magic land of Narnia, where Aslan the lion was the Son of the Great Emperor and ruled in peace and justice, the last battle was approaching. The bad seemed to outweigh the good, and little hope was left. Everyone who was not on the side of the bad, whether they were really on the side of the good or not, were afraid. The Dwarfs, especially. They were afraid to trust, afraid to take sides. So they did neither, except as regarded themselves. They sided with themselves, they trusted only in themselves, they were out only for themselves.

There are a lot of "Dwarfs" in our world, people who only trust in themselves, people who are only concerned with themselves. They are folk who make books like *Looking Out for Number One* and *Winning Through Intimidation* best sellers. They are people who are busy about getting on with their lives, who have little time for others' concerns or needs— they are far too consumed by their own problems. Oh, they might allow someone to walk with them for a way, if that person is willing to follow their rules. But basically, these people are concerned with private enterprise.

I think it's because they, like the Dwarfs, are afraid that if I don't look out for myself, no one else will; that if you want something done right, you gotta do it yourself. Fear. People can't be trusted or relied upon, and to keep from getting the shaft, one way or another, everything becomes a private endeavor. Always looking out for private interests, how things will affect *me* how it can be used to *my* advantage.

It's really sad, somehow.

Why?

Let's look back in on the Dwarfs again. After the last battle had been fought, and the forces of good, the forces of Aslan, had won the final victory, the old Narnia (the old world), passed away. But into the new Narnia (the new earth), into heaven, came all those from the old world who would. The gate to the new world was, oddly enough, a stable. To enter the new world, one entered the stable, but if, upon entering, you were willing to see, you were really not in a stable at all, but just on the other side of the door. The other side was "a beautifully new and fresh world where all was peace and joy. But the Dwarfs refused to see. They were in the dark, and would let no one lead them into light, even though the Narnia children tried to.

'All right!' said Eustace indignantly. 'We're not blind. We've got eyes in our heads.'

'They must be darn good ones if you can see in here,' said the same Dwarf whose name was Diggle.

'In where?' asked Edmund.

'Why you bone-head, in *here* of course,' said Diggle. 'In this pitch-black, poky, smelly little hole of a stable.'

'Are you blind?' said Tirian.

'Ain't we all blind in the dark?' said Diggle.

'But it isn't dark, you poor stupid Dwarfs,' said Lucy. 'Can't you see? Look up! Look round! Can't you see the sky and the trees and the flowers? Can't you see me?'

'How in the name of Humbug can I see what ain't there? And how can I see you any more than you can see me in this pitch darkness?'

'Oh the poor things!' said Lucy."[2] She tried to convince them that there was a wonderful, blessed world about them if they'd just care to look. But they wouldn't. The Dwarfs just looked at each other, always at themselves, never beyond. Their last word was, "We haven't let anyone take us in. The Dwarfs are for the Dwarfs."

So many people miss out on the richness of life because they are too concerned with themselves and their own interests. There are a lot of Christians like that. And they hurt themselves most of all—too selfish to love, to share, to enjoy. But the blessing of the Lord is that we may all look beyond ourselves to the beauty of loving others, the beauty of God's will, the beauty of service. Paul and Timothy were more concerned with others than themselves, more concerned with the cause of Christ than with their private affairs. They are the ones who ultimately found life fruitful.

Father,
Allow me to lose myself in you
   in your will
   in your people
   in your love,
Concerned more with you than me.
And in losing myself in you, let me find
   myself anew.
Caring as I should care,
Acting as I should act; busy not with incidentals,
   but with the ultimate things of life—
   your will
   your people
   your Son's purpose.

In whose name I pray,
Amen.

Misplaced Zeal

3:2-7

Beware of the dogs, beware of the evil workers, beware of the false circumcision; for we are the true circumcision, who worship in the Spirit of God and

*glory in Christ Jesus and put no confidence in the
flesh, although I myself might have confidence even
in the flesh. If anyone else has a mind to put confidence in the flesh, I far more: circumcised the eighth
day, of the nation of Israel, of the tribe of Benjamin,
a Hebrew of Hebrews; as to the Law, a Pharisee; as
to zeal, persecutor of the church; as to the righteousness which is in the Law, found blameless. But whatever things were gain to me, those things I have
counted loss for the sake of Christ (3:2-7, NASB).*

There is nothing more frightening than misplaced
zeal.

When I was a child, I remember seeing a filmclip
of Hitler addressing his troops. The little man in the
military uniform shouted and ranted. A torrent of
words spilled from his lips—words filled with hatred
and brimming with menace for the people of the
world. At each pause in his speech, his soldiers would
cheer, thundering their approval of his plans and
their dedication to the realization of those plans. In
the years of war that followed that speech, those
soldiers laid waste much of Europe in their zeal to
carry out the commands of their leader.

I am frightened when I realize the number of times
I have given myself zealously to the wrong things.
For example, I was once taken with a zeal for personal independence. Caught up in this pursuit, I
sometimes forsook others when they needed me
most. "No strings attached" was the condition that I
placed on all relationships. Now as I look back, I see
the casualties, the wounded that I left in the wake of
my passing. My misplaced zeal scarred the lives of
people who loved me. The destructive power of my
misplaced zeal is a frightening fact of life, a fact that
I must face, unless I wish to go on carelessly wreck-
ing havoc in the lives of people.

There is nothing more wasteful than misplaced zeal.

As teenagers, we plunge headlong into the scramble for status. We *must* become part of the right group. We *must* learn to speak the right way. As adults we continue this same quest for status. We *must* drive a certain type of car. We *must* live in a home like that of our friends. No matter that we may lose our own indentities in the process, becoming submerged in the uniformity of the group—we *must* become a part of the group regardless of the cost.

And so we play out the story of our lives, acting the roles in which we have cast ourselves. Often we come to the end of our lives only to find that we have never really lived. We have been only actors. We have forfeited our identities, all that might have made us unique and useful, in order to play at the game called "conformity." We have played the game with zeal and determination. But it has been, after all, only a game. And it has cost us our lives.

What gives rise to this blind allegiance to the wrong things? Misplaced zeal is born of misplaced confidence. In our pride, we think that we can shape and build our own lives without reference to God. We seek our identities in things, "in the flesh" to borrow Paul's words. So long as we continue to try and construct our lives by means of our own strength and wisdom, we shall succumb to the sin of misplaced zeal. We will be a danger to ourselves and to those around us.

There is only one way to deal with our problem. Casting aside all reservations, all pride, all hope in our own strength, we must enter into the love of Jesus Christ. Counting as loss all the things upon which we have based our identity, we must leap into the adventure of living in him. In Christ, we will find

ourselves and a direction for our zeal. Having found
ourselves, we will be free to exercise our gifts in worship of God and service to the world.

Father:
We confess to you that
we have been lost in our pride.
We have given ourselves to the world,
seeking our identities in things
of the flesh.
With misplaced zeal, we have sought for peace
where no peace may be found.
Forgive us our folly, we beseech you.
We come before you asking that
you lead us to Jesus Christ.
Help us to find ourselves
in the depths of his love.
Let our zeal, our energy,
be directed according to your will.
In the name of him who said,
"Not my will, but thine."

                                        Amen.

Knowing
3:8-11

*More than that, I count all things to be loss in view
of the surpassing value of knowing Christ Jesus my
Lord, for whom I have suffered the loss of all things,
and count them but rubbish in order that I may gain
Christ, and may be found in Him, not having a righteousness of my own derived from the Law, but that
which is through faith in Christ, the righteousness
which comes from God on the basis of faith, that I*

may know Him, and the power of His resurrection and the fellowship of His sufferings, being conformed to His death; in order that I may attain to the resurrection from the dead (3:8-11, NASB).

Lord, the other day I heard a man speak on "The Rewards of Knowing Jesus." He spoke well, and with words, painted pictures of the life with Christ for those of us who sat listening to him. According to this fellow, getting to know Jesus and taking out an insurance policy were about the same thing. If we would only get to know Jesus, we would be protected from the unexpected problems of life. "Knowing Jesus," he said, "was the single best way to discover the good life—a life of plenty, filled with fun, good times, and friends."

Lord, if that man had been selling cars, I would have bought one right then and there.

But he was not selling cars, Lord. He was trying to sell us on you—and I am not sure that he understood the product he was attempting to market. For that matter, I am not sure I really understood what was involved in knowing Jesus.

Can you help me?

"My child, there is a great deal involved in knowing Jesus. But the first and most important thing is this: Knowing Jesus is the single most crucial aspect of a human life. You do not seek to meet Jesus in order to gain for yourself earthly treasures or security. You seek Jesus in order to gain life itself! Without him, you are merely a shadow, an image with no substance, here one moment and gone the next. In him, you find shape and substance and meaning—you find life.

"There can be no casual relation between yourself and Jesus. It is all or nothing. When you come to Jesus, you throw in your lot with his lot. You go for broke. As he risked all that he had in obedience to God's will, so must you risk all. If you would experience the fellowship of his resurrection, you must be willing to experience the fellowship of his suffering. All of this is what it means to bear your cross. Real life always begins with death to self.

"My child, knowing Jesus is no easy task. True, there is untold joy in that fellowship; but there is also great risk. The friends of Jesus always run the chance of death on a cross. The choice is yours. Do you really want to know Jesus?"

Father, I think I want to know Jesus, but I am scared of the dangers, even as I am thrilled by the joys of discipleship. Please, Lord, hear now my prayer.

Oh, Lord God, Father of Jesus Christ,
you know the desire of my heart.
You have looked deep within my heart
and have seen my longing for your Son.
You have probed the mysteries of my thought
and have seen my doubt and fear.
Father, grant me . . .
a greater sense of my need for Jesus,
courage to follow the way of Jesus,
strength to finish what I have begun.
Father, take what I have;
help me to start where I am;
guide my feet until
I come face to face
with Jesus.
        Amen.

Five Finger Exercise
3:12,14-15

I do not claim that I have already succeeded or have already become perfect. I keep striving to win the prize for which Christ Jesus has already won me to himself . . . . So I run straight toward the goal in order to win the prize, which is God's call through Christ Jesus to the life above. All of us who are spiritually mature should have this same attitude. But if some of you have a different attitude, God will make this clear to you (3:12,14-15, GNB).

Five finger exercises in the young pianist's practice time carry no hint of great symphonies as yet unwritten. Five finger exercises are necessary, however, to the growth and development of young musical talent. Beethoven did not write the "Moonlight Sonata" before he learned to read music. And Handel wrote *The Messiah* only after he had learned to play in both major and minor keys.

How poor the world would be if Beethoven, Handel, and many other great musical talents had not developed through perseverance and practice. If these great musicians had stopped maturing musically—or if they had become "contented" artistically, even if they had "given-up" personally—the world would be a less beautiful place.

But what has that got to do with us?

What was true for Beethoven and Handel is also true for us. Oh, not that all of us will be composers of music, although some of us may be with practice and perseverance. But their lessons teach us in a different way. Just like playing scales, having sore hands, and hitting occasional sour notes are part of the process of becoming a good pianist, the Christian must develop and mature in his faith.

The Christian life is a life of growth. "Press toward the mark" is the way Paul spoke of it in 3:14. In our pilgrimage we need to "play the scales," as we attempt to read the gospel and make it our own. We must have "sore hands," from attempting to live out our faith in the world. Inevitably, we will play sour notes—hurting those we love, letting standards slip as we often forget the "high calling of God."

All the struggle and all the pain—but mostly, all the growth—is a part of maturing as a Christian. We, like the young pianist, must learn to play in the major and minor keys of the gospel. But many folk forget that Christian growth is for all Christians. Many older Christians become stagnant, thinking they have arrived. But Paul said no to this understanding. Here he was, perhaps the greatest Christian of all time, saying in effect, "I press on. I haven't gotten there yet. I'm not perfect, but I keep trying." All of us need to reflect his awareness in our own lives as we press on. Knowing that we are not perfect, we still must keep on practicing, keep on learning, keep on going in accordance with God's will for our lives.

God, through Jesus Christ has done his part. He has won us to himself through his life, death, and resurrection. But that is no license for us to relax, we must be good stewards of his grace to us. We become good stewards by attempting, trying, struggling, becoming.

Almighty God, help us celebrate our being by
    becoming—
  all that we can be,
  all that you mean us to be,
knowing that what we are is your gift to us,
but that what we become is our gift to you.
                          Amen.

Life in the Present Tense
3:13

Of course, my brothers, I really do not think that I have already won it; the one thing I do, however, is to forget what is behind me and do my best to reach what is ahead" (3:13, GNB).

"I guess she just never got over Bob's death," Mrs. Jones' daughter told me recently. "She still cries everyday. Everytime she looks at his picture or sees something of his, like his glasses, she breaks down again. She's left his bedroom exactly like it was before he died. She still goes to all the places they went. She goes to the cemetery three or four times a week. She even resents friends' attempts at cheering her up. It's almost like she wants to continue grieving. All she's doing is living in the past."

Mrs. Jones is only one among many in our world who live in the past. Many people live in the past, however, most in even subtler ways. Some people surround themselves with old things so that they never have to notice that today is a new day. Some people go on nostalgia crazes, trying to capture the magic of days gone by. Some consider the good ole days the only days that ever were good.

Now there is nothing wrong with appreciating the past. How unfortunate persons we would be if we lived only in the present, isolated from our traditions and culture! However, the revering of the past to the exclusion of today is very unhealthy. In fact, an attitude like this can be very dangerous. Our institutions for the mentally ill are full of persons who are unable to deal with the present, with today, with the real world. Newspapers and television tell us sad stories of people whose lives end tragically because they could not come to grips with today.

Christians, at times, fall prey to retreating from today. New songs, new versions of the Bible, new styles of preaching, new forms of church architecture—even new orders of service for worship—all are very threatening to these Christians. The old and familiar—the places where we've already been—are safe. There are usually few surprises lurking in the familiar.

But just as living too much in the past can be emotionally damaging for all persons, living too much in the religious past is dangerous for Christians. The gospel is God's good news to every "today's" person. It is not confined to yesterday's people, places, and forms, but ever new, ever ready to burst forth onto man's need for God.

We must use our past. But we must also look to what is here now, as well as what is to come.

Paul said that he kept looking forward, running to the goal ahead. He remembered the past—both the good and the not so good. But the past never shackled his life or his mission. His life was now, today. He looked forward to his life in the future. And his mission was ever present. I get the image of the drill sergeant snapping at the recruit, "Eyes to the front, soldier!" Exactly! Knowing where we come from, and using all the lessons the past teaches, we must look ahead and move there. And we move, not fearing the future, but confident that God's Spirit will guide us.

Press on. Live the Christian life. Live it in the present tense. Keep your eyes to the front. Know where you've been, but know, too, where you are and where you're headed.

Lord,

Help me be aware when I retreat to the past.

But help me know that when I have retreated,

I can move ahead anew.
Help me celebrate today as a new gift from you,
    a new creation to be used.
Help me be contemporary, living the age-old faith
    in ever-new days and ways.
                                        Amen.

A Good Example
3:17-19

Keep on imitating me, my brothers. Pay attention to those who follow the right example that we have set for you. I have told you this many times before, and now I repeat it with tears: there are many whose lives make them enemies of Christ's death on the cross. They are going to end up in hell, because their god is their bodily desires. They are proud of what they should be ashamed of, and they think only of things that belong to this word (3:17-19, GNB).

An Example

Johann Gutenberg did a great thing in the Rhineland of Germany in the 1440s. He developed the printing press. Before that time, if you wanted a copy of something, you sat down and copied it—by hand.

There are two problems with copying something by hand: one, it takes a very long time; and two, if your handwriting is anything like mine, once you have your copy, there are certain times when you're not sure what your copy says.

But that's what it took. Before moveable type, before typewriters, before Xerox, there were people who had to copy documents if the documents were going to be preserved. The kinds of documents ranged from business records to the Bible. And it was all very important. The copyist had to be very careful to copy everything correctly. And the people that wanted the copying done were picky. Churches wanted their copies of Scripture error-free, and businessmen, then as now, wanted their records exact. Therefore, not just everyone could do the copying.

It was like that in Jesus' time as well. The scribes mentioned in the Bible were very important people. They had been to school to learn to copy the Law correctly. And until Gutenberg, the procedure was generally the same. Men who would be copyists, or scribes, went to school to learn the proper way of writing.

In school, the master scribe would give the apprentice a piece of paper with the letters E-X-A-M-P-L-E written across the top. Those letters contained every "stroke" that the copyist would have to make. The young copyist would have to master the printing of those letters. He literally had to follow the "example" set before him. After he had followed the example enough times, the stroke of the pen came naturally for him.

Not all of us are copyists, but all of us follow examples. The examples we follow develop the natural strokes for our lives. We personally choose the examples we will follow. These examples play a large part in making us who we are.

We are Christians. We need to follow good examples in learning the strokes of Christian living. Paul told us to follow his example. But what did he mean? Didn't he just say that he had no righteousness of his own (3:9)?

Paul encouraged us to follow the example of relying totally upon God's grace and righteousness. We will fall short of what we should be as Christians. But when we rely on God for strength and allow him to be our righteousness, we are following the right example.

Lord, allow me to rely more on grace than
  strength,
following the example of Paul's total surrender
  to your will.   Amen.

Enemies

In J. R. R. Tolkien's *Lord of the Rings,* we read of a land called Middle-earth. In some ways, it is not a very good place to find yourself, for there is a war going on. The Enemy is attempting to conquer Middle-earth. On his side are the Orcs (horrible creatures!), the Trolls, the Goblins, and the Darkness.

Against the Enemy are aligned the Men, the Hobbits, the Elves, and the Dwarves. They fight great battles, an many are killed before the end. Yet, in all the confusion of the war there is one great blessing: you can always tell the good guys from the bad. The lines are clearly drawn.

Alas! For such clarity in our own world. But in our world, the good guys often are bad guys, too, and sometimes the bad guys can be the good guys.

The one place that the good ought to always be good, though, and the bad always bad, is the church. Sad to say, there has been a lot of evil done in the name of the church—racism, oppression, cheating, backbiting all from those who claim the example of Jesus! And all that we do which is not in accordance with the will of God through the example of Jesus makes us enemies of the cross.

Interesting we could almost say that the only people who can be enemies of the cross are those who know the cross. Only those who are in the church can be enemies of the cross. Others might deny God or try to prevent the witness of the church from spreading. But Judas was the traitor. Only those who know of the meaning of the cross can deny the meaning of the cross in their lives. And denying the impact of the cross in our lives is what Paul called being an enemy of Christ's death on the cross.

Only we in the church can be enemies of the cross. For if we know what the death of Jesus means, and how it should transform our lives, and still live as if the cross made no difference, we are then far worse than those who never knew.

Holy Father,

Even those of us who love you best often find ourselves as enemies of your Son's death on the cross.

For we allow that which should transform us to affect us not. And our sin, then, is not so much commission as it is omission—omitting from our experience and practice the grace which you have shown to us through your Son's sacrifice.

Forgive us when we actively prohibit your will—through insensitivity, oppression, bigotry, slander, malice.

But forgive us, too, when we simply don't let your Word affect our living. And move to transform us anew, so that our lives may follow, as well as be, a good example.

Through Christ our Lord,

Amen.

Improper Perspective

You can look at almost anything any number of ways. Perspective, though, is the key to any avenue of life. We've all heard the "half-empty, half-full" story. The point being, the difference between an optimist and a pessimist is the *way* they look at things.

How can we tell the difference between a Christian and anyone else? Through love, Jesus said. Through their perspective, Paul said. This is another way of saying what Jesus said.

A Christian celebrates life, joy, love, helping his neighbor, progress in international relations, a person coming to Christ, and forsaking all for the sake of the gospel.

Anybody else celebrates themselves—their bellies, their closets, their bank accounts, their garages, their positions. Anyone can be "anybody." Only one who has heard the Word of God can be a Christian.

I am often "anybody else," proud of what anybody can be proud of, ashamed of humility and service.

Lord, help me to be a Christian, and not just "anybody else."

I know that I shall not be better than anyone else, for being a Christian is not attaining—it is giving. I shall not be better, just better informed.

A Good Example

One of the most truly Christian men I ever knew once said, "I'm not a Christian. Not really. I know what the New Testament says. But I get a *'D-'* in doing what is written. Jesus said that the one who has two coats should give one to the one without. The last time I looked, I had more than one coat in my closet." It's tough trying to be a Christian.

I agree. It's tough trying to follow the examples of Jesus and Paul—not to mention all the saints and sinners who have lived and died and those who live today. But being a Christian—and not just believing, but doing—comes with time, the will to follow, and following the right examples. Each day we must allow the examples of Jesus and Paul to become more and more our standards of life. Our examples.

They show us the right strokes.

We must write our lives by their examples.

Dear God,

We pray to be not only believers in, but practitioners of your gospel.

We pray to have courage to allow our faith to make a difference in our lives.

We pray to be overwhelmed by your power for our lives,

So that we do what is right, and that our fruits are unspoiled by the taint of worldly greed or malice.

We pray to be more like Paul, even as he prayed to be more like Jesus,

Even in whose name we pray,
Amen.

The Way to Stand Firm
4:1-6,8-9*a*

So then, my brothers, how dear you are to me and how I miss you! How happy you make me, and how proud I am of you!—this, dear brothers, is how you should stand firm in your life in the Lord. Euodia and Syntyche, please, I beg you, try to agree as sisters in the Lord. And you too, my faithful partner, I want you to help these women; for they have worked hard with me to spread the gospel, together with Clement and all my other fellow workers, whose names are in God's book of the living. May you always be joyful

in your union with the Lord. I say it again: rejoice!
Show a gentle attitude toward everyone. The Lord is
coming soon. Don't worry about anything, but in all
your prayers ask God for what you need, always ask-
ing with a thankful heart. In conclusion, my
brothers, fill your minds with those things that are
good and that deserve praise: things that are true,
noble, right, pure, lovely, and honorable. Put into
practice what you learned and received from me,
both from my words and from my actions
(4:1-6,8-9, GNB).

When I was in college, a time came when I had to
decide what direction my life would take. There were
lots of possibilities—medicine, music, law, or theology. All were things that interested me. But I
couldn't make up my mind. So I made no firm decisions about anything. Kind of plodded along was
what I did.

My supervisor called me in one day, and being a
friend as well as a professor, asked what I was going
to do. I told him that I still wasn't sure. I wanted to
do everything, to give up nothing. All he said was,
"Remember—you can't do it all. And every discipline exacts its own toll."

The confusion of those days is past now. But I still
remember my friend's words, "Every discipline
exacts its own toll." And he was right. No matter the
endeavor, one has to pay the price.

—The football player works his body into a finely
tuned machine, one that will perform in the game,
through hard physical regimen.

—The scholar spends countless hours in the library
perusing books and texts which are often dusty
with age and disuse.

—The medical doctor learns chemistry, anatomy,
physiology, and medicine—so that he'll be able to

prescribe the right medicine when bodies are sick. Every field has its own ideals, ethics, morals, and discipline of study. And the price always has to be paid for excellence in the field.

Christianity is a discipline. All who will be good Christians must do those things necessary to honor the high calling of God through his Son, Jesus. It takes work, hard work; and it's not easy. Real doctors not only know the names of various medicines but they also understand the medicine's composition, how it works, and when to prescribe it. Authentic Christians not only know all the right words and phrases—Jesus is Lord, the grace of God, persevering in the faith—but they also know the truth of each. For all of the phrases mean something which impacts their experience.

Paul spoke here of "standing firm" in our life in the Lord. But what does that mean? Paul would say to us that to know how to stand firm in the gospel must include knowing how:

—to agree. Unity is the keynote of Christian fellowship, brothers and sisters united in love and common cause. Church should not be a group of people where, as a pastor recently summed up much church life, "they just got through fighting, are in a fight now, or are about to start." Unity is the ingredient in all that matters and tolerance and love above all else.

—to be gentle. The Christian is courteous, noble, generous, kind, not violent, harsh, or rough. A Christian should really smile and love. He is one who is understanding and patient.

—to be joyous. Joy is not emotion alone. Joy is a perspective through which we view life. It is a lens that allows us to see all that is in light of God's love, forgiveness, and will. Being joyous is being childlike—no matter our age—and fascinated by the ordinary.

—to be thankful. It's a cliche to say in November "everyday should be Thanksgiving." It's the Christian who can be thankful for the ever-new within the ever-present. If "genius" is "shooting at something no one else can see, and hitting it,"[3] then Christian thanks is gratefulness for the not so apparent in the knowledge that our eyes are sometimes dim.

Standing firm in the Lord includes all those things —unity, gentleness, joy, thankfulness. But it's more. Standing firm is doing, in any situation, that which is true to God's design in that situation. Our guidelines are sometimes limited. To stand firm is to do whatever is right and filling one's mind with those things which are true, good, lovely, deserving of praise, honorable, and of God.

Heavenly Father,

Help us to stand firm in the faith—through commitment to you, sensitivity to our brothers and sisters.

Unity with God and man.

Joyous as children. Thankful and gentle.

In all we do.

Through Christ our Lord,
Amen.

The Strength of Christ
4:13

I have the strength to face all conditions by the power that Christ gives me (4:13, GNB).

The great German pastor and theologian, Helmut Thielicke, tells how, early in his ministry, he decided to take seriously the words of Jesus, "All power is given unto me in heaven and in earth." He acted upon his faith in the overcoming power of Christ, that in the final analysis nothing could stand before the strength of the Almighty.[4]

His faith in Jesus' words did not go untested. Early in Thielicke's ministry, the power of Adolf Hitler and his merciless war machine reached its pinnacle. It was hard to believe what Jesus had said. On the set of the radio station from which he broadcast sermons, Thielicke was aided by "two very old ladies and a still older man. He was a very worthy man, but his fingers were palsied and this was embarrassingly apparent in his playing."

He continued, "So this was the extent of the accomplishment of this Lord, to whom all power in heaven and earth had been given, supposedly given. And outside marched the battalions of (Hitler) youth who were subject to altogether different lords. This was all he had to set before me on that evening. What *did* he have to offer anyway?"[5]

Thielicke's doubts invade us all at times. The faith-assertion of the power and goodness of God at times seems shaky under the weight of the awareness of war, hunger, evil. And not only that but also it is seemingly the bad guy who wins—always, and in spite of God. David saw it:

But as for me, my feet had almost stumbled,
    my steps had well nigh slipped.
For I was envious of the arrogant,
    When I saw the prosperity of the wicked.
Behold, these are the wicked;
    always at ease, they increase in riches.
All in vain I have kept my heart clean

and washed my hands in innocence.
(Ps. 73:2-3,12-13, RSV).

David, along with the young Thielicke and many of us, saw that the strength of God is sometimes absent when it is most needed.

Or is that really what we see? Could it be that our point of reference is faulty? Power to us is the A-bomb. Is that a worthy comparison to God's power? The Jews expected a military messiah—a king in strength and glory. But instead of a warrior, a Prince of Peace came unto them. Strong he was, indeed. But not strong in the clash of weapons or in the noise of open battle. Jesus was strong in devotion and most powerful of all in his silence before Pilate.

We would wish that God would cure all cancer, eradicate Marxist Communism, do away with hunger, disaster, and injustice. We would like the vengeful strength of God to be shown, and very mightily, against all who are lined up opposite us.

But God's strength seldom works that way; evil often falls of its own weight eventually. Usually, instead of fighting for us as we watch, he strengthens us to fight for ourselves. God's strength is not always found in armies of angels. God's strength is found in the consoling, the uplifting, and the strengthening of his people—like you and me.

Paul was arrested, beaten, stoned—probably killed. Yet he rang out that God strengthened him. Strength, not in force or vengeance. But strength of Spirit and purpose.

In the face of our world, we might ask for A-bombs. God gives us himself instead. And at that moment, Buechner says, we look like persons who have asked for a crust but have been given instead the whole loaf of bread. For we are not given merely what God does—but God himself.[6]

Father,
Strength of our souls, power of our existence,
Help us find your power not according to the
    world's standards—
    but in peace instead of war
    in joy rather than bawdiness
    in silence rather than the noise of conflict
Help us, because of the strength of you in us,
to do all we can as your instruments
to rely on the Spirit
to face all situations with hope—
not the hope of vindication, but the hope of love
    and peace.
Even as your strength works out your will.
                    Through Christ our Lord,
                    Amen.

Abundance of Blessings
4:18-19

*Here, then, is my receipt for everything you have
given me—and it has been more than enough! I have
all I need now that Epaphroditus has brought me all
your gifts. These are like a sweet-smelling offering to
God, a sacrifice which is acceptable and pleasing to
him. And with all his abundant wealth through
Christ Jesus, my God will supply all your needs
(4:18-19, GNB).*

"It's not fair!" he screamed as he burst into the
house. His scream—maybe it was more of a
screech—rudely called me back to reality. I was supposed to be baby-sitting for my sister. What I had
done, actually, was to stretch out on the couch, turn

on the ballgame, and drift into that half-awake/half-asleep "twilight zone" I liked so much. And I wasn't worried about the kids. Every boy and girl in the neighborhood had convened to play wiffle-ball in the backyard. Simple enough, right? A nice, easy, pick-up game of wiffle-ball while the old major-leaguer had a nice, leisurely seventh-inning "stretch" on the couch.

The bellow from my nephew ended that fantasy.

I sat bolt-upright, sure that the four horsemen of the Apocalypse had just ridden through and I had missed it. The cobwebs began to clear, and he was still screaming, crying too. His was not a blubbery, sad cry, a mad, frustrated cry—like he'd just been in a fight.

"Hold on a minute, Bill. What's the matter? Quit crying. Now what's the problem?"

"It's not fair! They don't play fair! Those big guys don't pay any attention to the rules! They let the girls have ten strikes, not three. And they drop balls on purpose so they can get on base. Then they let the girls score. We haven't got a chance! It's just not fair!"

"But Bill—it's just for fun. And isn't it nice to let the girls get into the game a little more? They *are* your sisters, you know. Don't you want them to have a good time?"

"Rules are rules, and it's *not fair!*"

My nephew's concern with fairness is understandable. Most of us are concerned in one way or another with what's fair. We want everything fair. Our society is built upon that notion:

—"Liberty and justice for all."

—"One man, one vote."

—"An honest day's work for an honest day's pay."

We have been concerned to legislate equality (fairness) and civil rights for minorities and women. We are upset if people are treated unfairly.

Much of the reality of our world is governed by concerns for fairness. Our concerns find religious root in the Old Testament. Justice and equality are primary issues. "An eye for an eye and a tooth for a tooth"—that's about as fair as you can be. And God relates to people much the same way.

Thus says the Lord:

"For three trangressions of Gaza,
and for four, I will not revoke
the punishment because they carried into exile a
whole people to deliver them up to Edom.
So I will send a fire upon the wall of Gaza,
and it shall devour her strongholds"
(Amos 1:6-7, RSV).

That's only fair, isn't it? We sin. We get punished. It's fair.

The New Testament paints a slightly different picture, however. Paul wrote to us that God is not so concerned with fairness as he is with grace. Let us be thankful. For in Paul's words, "All have sinned . . . . for the wages of sin is death" (Rom. 3:23; 6:23). If God were only being fair, giving to sinners exactly as they deserve, we would all be under the judgment of death.

But God gives to us. He gives freely. And that's what grace is. "Justified by his grace as a gift" (Rom. 3:24, RSV). A gift, given by God, to undeserving recipients. God's love for us overshadowed the fairness of punishment.

Paul knew this grace of God, the grace which gives, and continues giving. As he thanked the Philippians for their gifts, he was at the same time thankful to God for his grace.

That says something to me, something very important.

—Often we are the instruments of God's grace to others. Our prayers, our gifts, our love, and our attitudes show our God to those around us. And when we fail to be instruments of grace, we not only fail God but we also fail our brothers and sisters.

—Giving in material ways and spiritual ways is blessed. Not only is giving a blessed thing to do but also it is an action which God blesses in return.

—God's grace not only saves us but also sustains us day to day.

Father—

Help me to be graceful
    in attitude, in action, in regard for others.

Help me to give freely,
    not concerned with getting in return or being
    paid back;
    not concerned with justice, or whether people
    deserve my gifts,

But help me give freely
    because you have given freely to me in grace
    because I long to be an instrument of that grace
to others.

Help me go the extra mile.

Help me give the extra dollar.

Help me to swallow the easy rebuke.

Help me forgive, even as I have been forgiven
    by you.

Showing my love for you, the one who loves most
    freely, to all who need you.

                    Because of Christ our Lord,
                    Amen.

III
Community and Joy

Partners

1:5

*Thankful for your partnership in the gospel from
the first day until now (1:5, RSV).*

To be a living thing in God's universe one has to
give and receive. Biology teaches us this basic prin-
ciple. We need air to live, as do plants. As we
breathe, our lungs use the oxygen and exhale the car-
bon dioxide. Plants, on the other hand, use the car-
bon dioxide and expel the oxygen. Thus, we live in
perfect "partnership," providing for each other's
needs. The universe is built upon partnership and
community.

An old story is told of a man who dreamed one
night he had moved into the next world. He was
given a vision of heaven and hell. The angel who took
him on this tour told him that death affected people
in only one way. Other than that, people were just
the same as they had been in this life. The one difference was that death stiffened people's elbows.

The angel took the man first on a tour of hell.
There was a scene of unbelievable confusion and
hostility. People had abundant food in their hands.
But because of their stiff arms, they couldn't get the
food to their mouths. They were completely frustrated. Everyone was angrily knocking everyone else
down as they futilely attempted to meet their own
needs.

Then the man was taken on a tour of heaven. In
heaven, people's elbows were just as stiff as they
were in hell. But in heaven, the atmosphere was com-

pletely different. There was joy and harmony and a great sense of community. The people in heaven had found a solution to their problem. Instead of thinking only of themselves, they concentrated also on the needs of others. There they were, paired off face-to-face, each feeding and being fed by one another.

A developing, maturing Christian salvation involves both giving and receiving. This is the essence of true partnership. There is no better example of this kind of partnership than the relationship shared between the Philippian church and Paul. Paul gave to them, out of a loving heart, the very gospel of Jesus Christ. And in return, the Philippians continually aided Paul in the ongoing of his missionary work.

We, as Christians, receive life from God and must, as partners, give back the contribution of devoted service. Let us pray this prayer:

Father of our Lord Jesus Christ:
Thankful we are for the gift of the gospel,
    for redemption both now and forever,
    for joy, peace, and love,
    for fellowship,
Help us to celebrate the gift by giving
    to those around us whom we know not,
    as well as to those whom we do;
    to our brothers and sisters in Christ,
    as to all we encounter.
True partners with our brothers and sisters.
Help us to live out your mission on earth,
    going where he went,
    speaking to whom he spoke,
    and knowing the reasons why,
True partners with you forever more.
                    Amen.

Fight Together
1:27

Now, the important thing is that your way of life should be as the gospel of Christ requires, so that, whether or not I am able to go to see you, I will hear that you are standing firm with one common purpose that with only one desire you are fighting together for the faith of the gospel (1:27, GNB).

"We must stop giving the impression that the church is surrounded by a wall, fighting for its existence against a world that is trying to destroy it; instead, we must realize that the church is a force pushing out into the world."[1]

Force. Power. Strength. The church of God should be all three things, and in some ways it is. Henry Steele Commager said, "Certainly, by every test but that of influence, the church has never been stronger. Its membership is growing more rapidly than the population. The increase in wealth and in social activities is even more impressive. Never before has the church been materially more powerful, or spiritually less effective.[2]

The power of the church of God should be in its influence, in its prophetic role toward the wrongs of society. Sadly, much of church life is a sanctioning of the status quo. Jesus meant for his church to provide a witness, a voice—a voice which both calls people in and a voice that goes out to challenge and correct. A church of action, in other words.

The Council of Trent said it this way, "The Church consists primarily of two parts, the one called Church triumphant, the other called Church militant."

"So what's the problem?" said one of my ladies to

me. "We're militant. You ought to know, you've been in our business sessions!"

That's precisely the problem. The fighting the church ought to do, the moving out in the name of Christ, has gradually been replaced by fighting among parishioners or groups and a settling-in of concerns.

Paul said we ought to stand united in common cause and fight for the sake of the gospel—providing light for those around us to see. Our light should shine in the darkness of men's understanding and reflect the Son of God. But most of our fighting produces more heat than light. There is the tendency to waste time, energy, and vitality—not to mention creative thought—on bickering and quarreling.

This ought not to be so!

The quest for the church is to find the strength, power, and force which the Holy Spirit gives to us, and use all that he gives for the "moving-out" we need to do. The church as a whole must stand firm, call out to those who need the love of God, preach against that which the church shouldn't sanction— fight for the faith. Unity. Strength. Influence. Militant, and triumphant. The church ought to do all that, be all that.

But that will only happen in the corporate when it happens in the individual. We must be all those things for the church to be so. For the church is people, people like you and me. We must begin again to reestablish our priorities, to find within us the unity and strength and common purpose which the Spirit grants and of which Paul speaks.

We must call in and move out.

We must stand in union.

We must be militant, but not with each other, producing light more than heat.

For we are the church.

"The church is never a place, but always a people; never a fold but always a flock, never a sacred building but always a believing assembly. The church is you who pray, not where you pray. A structure of brick or marble can no more be a church than your clothes . . . can be you. There is in this world nothing sacred but man, no sanctuary of God but the soul (Anonymous).[4]

How can you make the church what it ought to be?

Pray, work, love, believe, unite, witness, build, befriend, hope, and stand firm.

May God help each of us be his church.

The Mercy of God
2:27

Indeed he was ill, near to death. But God had mercy on him, and not only on him but on me also, lest I should have sorrow upon sorrow (2:27, RSV).

There is therefore now no condemnation for those who are in Christ Jesus. For the law of the Spirit of life in Christ Jesus has set me free from the law of sin and death (Rom. 8:1-2, RSV).

Lord, have mercy upon me, for I am a sinner.

The list of my sins is long, Lord. I have committed open and secret sins, small and great sins, sins of the flesh and sins of the spirit. Anger has spoken through my mouth so many times, bringing tears and confused pain to the eyes of those who love me. Pride has often placed its seal upon my lips so that I might not humble myself before others, make apologies, and receive and give forgiveness. Selfishness has blinded my eyes to the needs of those around me. I have stumbled forward in a darkness of my own making, seeking the treasures that have captured my heart, trampling lives beneath my unfeeling feet. I have sinned, oh Lord, more times than I can count; and the burden of guilt weighs heavy on me.

And I am afraid, Lord. For I know that I shall do these things again and again—and again. I don't want to hurt people; I don't want to add to my guilt—but I know that I will do so; and I am afraid as I stand alone, waiting for my next failure.

For I am more frightened of what I have discovered deep within myself, Lord, than of what I might do. I have long known that I commit sins, and that knowledge has been bad enough. But today I have looked into the deepest parts of my heart and found there an ancient darkness. I have let down buckets into the wells of my soul and have drawn them up only to find them filled with night.

I *am* a sinner, Lord! Despite my best intentions, regardless of my best efforts, there is a part of me that stands in open rebellion against you. And I, therefore, stand condemned before you, not for what I have done or will do, but for what I am.

Lord, have mercy upon me, for I am a sinner.

"Mercy I have, and mercy I give to you, my child. Since first you came to be, I have watched you with my eyes, eyes that see deeper into your soul than you will ever go. I, too, have seen that part of you that incites you to sin, that part of you that defies me and my Law.

"I have felt your pain as you struggled to understand why you felt the things that you felt and did the things that you did—I have suffered with you. Your frustrations have been my frustrations; your little successes, my joy; and your failures, my pain.

"Often, I have longed to touch you with healing so that you might be made whole. I have wanted to make you mine, giving myself to you and immersing your life within my life. I have desired to throw open the shutters of your heart and let the light of my love shine into every corner of your personality, banishing the darkness that has held you in thrall.

"But I could do none of these things until you asked me. I could not destroy the old evil within you until you saw that it was there, despaired of your own strength, and asked mercy of me. I could not, and cannot, batter down the door to your heart; but I can and will enter gladly the door opened by your hand.

"I am coming into your life now. I bring mercy, forgiveness, and strength as my gifts to you. Together, we shall fight the good fight; we shall change you and make of you a child of God."

Repeating the Great Truths
3:1

In conclusion, my brothers, be joyful in your union with the Lord. I don't mind repeating what I have written before, and you will be safer if I do so" (3:1, GNB).

Probably the most famous question of the New Testament is found in the context of Jesus' trial. Jesus stood, barely stood, before Pilate. A disheveled and rejected man—one would hardly have recognized him as a king—stood before the power and glory of Rome's finest. A sad scene, to be sure. But kind of funny, in an ironic sort of way. The procurator, in all his might, asked the carpenter's Son, "But what is truth?"

For centuries we have accused Pilate of cynicism and sarcasm. It has occurred to me that maybe he really wanted to hear what the truth was. The truth he knew was not truth at all. For empires fall; Caesars, who were called gods, died; and life plodded along. Pilate, like most of us, had learned to live around the absence of real truth. He lived in expediency—just doing what he needed to do to get by. As he saw Jesus, perhaps he looked into his eyes, and looking, perhaps Pilate was moved to ask his question because maybe, just perhaps, Jesus knew the answer.

Pilate asked. But Jesus didn't answer the question. He just stood there.

Jesus didn't answer. He was the answer. Jesus does not so much tell truth as he is the truth. And the truth is always fresh, always worth repeating, always enabling and strengthening. That's who Jesus is for the Christian and what he does. He's eternally new, even as he is the Ancient of Days, and his ageless newness is fresh and refreshing. We hear all the stories again, for in them there's always more to hear. The truth in Jesus always strengthens us.

Paul's writings bear witness to Christ as the truth. And he spoke of that Truth often. Paul said that writing again, or repeating, truth is no bother. Indeed it is a joy because the truths of the gospel are always fresh, newly true and significant, and strengthening. To repeat the truth of who Jesus is strengthens both the teller and the hearer.

Pilate wanted the truth but not enough to see it when it was right in front of him. Aren't we the same way? We've heard the truth enough to know it's there, and we even know where to seek it. But like Pilate, the concern is expediency. The truth calls us to real truth—in living, in relationship, in witness.

But real truth will get you hung on a cross, at times, even as truth himself was hung.

We're not truth. Nor are most of us much like him. But if we repeat the story, if we allow ourselves to hear again the Word of truth, then we are brought closer to him. We are strengthened. Knowing the Truth is knowing how far we fall short. But it is also experiencing the grace and joy that the Truth gives us. The grace and joy of forgiveness and peace. And hope—that there will be time when we will be servants of the Truth, bearers of good news. And we bear witness to the Truth through repeating that truth.

For those of us who have encountered Jesus as the Truth, the repeating is refreshing to us, and to all who hear.

Father,
We want to know the truth, to know
    intimately the living truth which we
    encounter in Christ Jesus.
For to know the Truth is to somehow live
    the truth—
Not in any perfected way. How often we fall, and
    how miserably we bear witness to his love!
    And for those sins we repent, asking
forgiveness.
But Father, we know that through your grace
    and love we have been called to hear the
    truth in your Son, and in hearing, to know
    the joy of God's truth.
Help us to hear anew each day, through
    the Word and ministers of the Word,
    the freshness, agelessness, and power of
    the truth.
And in hearing to be renewed, refreshed,
    strengthened.
To experience that joy unto the end that we share

the joy you give us in sweet abundance.
Grant to us, so that you may use us to grant unto
others.

> Through Christ our Lord.
> Amen.

Citizens of Heaven
3:20

We, however, are citizens of heaven, and we eagerly await for our Savior, the Lord Jesus Christ to come from heaven (3:20, GNB).

There the preacher stood, in all his piety. Sincere to be sure. But I heard him say it—with my own ears.

"And brethren, come that ole glory day when we all get to heaven, we will stand in heaven's great choirloft, and for the rest of the ages we will sing 'Amazing Grace.' We will sing the praises of the beloved Lamb of God forever."

Now God knows I love him. But he also knows I don't enjoy singing that much, that my voice cracks, and that I have trouble standing for great lengths of time. That old saint's view of heaven just doesn't square with mine. The thoughts of heaven being one long church service turns me off. When that day comes, there will be little of the old with which to compare it. But some things are clear.

We will be with God, his Son, and his Spirit.

We will know and in knowing, understand. All that was. All that is.

We will have responsibilities (cf. Matt. 25:14 ff.).

We will have eternal life.

Other than that, no one is sure. The author of Revelation used the best imagery at his disposal, and it all fell short. Paul's vision of heaven prompted him to proclaim that it was unlawful to even try to repeat what he saw. Only in the future will we ourselves see it as it is.

Yet, our presence in the kingdom, our citizenship in heaven, is present as well as future. Paul said we are (present tense) citizens of heaven. That means that though the glory of Christ's return is yet to be, still part of what heaven is about is already with us. Already we are residents in the kingdom. How so?

—Our lives are to be lived in the presence of the Father, in fellowship with the Son, guided by the Spirit.

—Though our knowledge and understanding are limited, we are at least aware of the magnitude of God's wisdom, as we participate in God's will.

—We have responsibilities in God's kingdom now to do justice and love mercy, Micah said. To be the salt of the earth, Jesus said. To love, even as we're loved.

—And our eternal life is already upon us. Eternal life is qualitative, as much as quantitative. The span of time may come up short this side of Jordan, but living life eternally, reflecting heaven in our attitude, is something we do here.

Yes, we are citizens of heaven now. And we are future residents of that great city. Now, and not yet. The kingdom both is, and is to be.

Father of heaven and Earth,
Help us be good citizens of heaven, even as we live
    the kingdom here
Looking forward to your coming at that day.
            Through the Prince of Peace we pray,
            Amen.

The Peace of God
4:7, 9a

And God's peace, which is far beyond human understanding, will keep your hearts and minds safe in union with Christ Jesus . . . . and the God who gives us peace will be with you (4:7,9, GNB).

I guess you could say that I stormed into the house. It had been a terrible day. My alarm had not sounded, and I had been late for class. When I did get to class, a test was being given for which I had forgotten to study. A professor-friend had broken a lunch date. The coffee machine was broken. Most everything I considered "nailed-down" had come loose. The day started, proceeded, and ended badly.

As I stormed into the house, I met my wife who had also had a bad day. Our meeting did nothing to soothe either one of us. A terrible day! No peace anywhere! I bet you have had days like that.

I went outside to think, to settle down, and to pray. I needed some peace, some order. I remembered about the "peace of God," and I wanted some. After all, after a day like mine, if there was anyone who deserved some peace, it was me!

As I reflected on the day, my mind drifted aimlessly. I thought of the news of the day—wars and revolution, nuclear dangers, displaced persons, starvation, floods. For some reason, I could think of nothing but the bad news (maybe because my mood was so bad).

As my thoughts turned away from myself, I felt strangely at ease. My woes over the coffee machine were rather meaningless when compared with the plight of starving children. Thinking of the troubles of others, I felt at peace.

But wait!!! That couldn't be the peace of God. The peace of God had nothing to do with glorying in the pain of others. I felt guilty because I was thinking *"Lord, how lucky that I am not going hungry or having a war fought in my backyard."* I realized how much I sounded like the Pharisee in Luke 18:9-14 (Read this story and think if you, too, ever sound like him).

Then what is the peace of God?

It must have something to do with our outlook on life. Paul said the peace of God allowed him to be satisfied with what he had in any situation (Phil. 4:11). The peace of God, then, allows us to see every situation with wisdom.

—We can see if something is really important or not, whether it is worth troubling with.

—We can see the places where we should place our attempts to do God's will.

—We can know that no matter what happens, God is working in every situation to redeem.

God's peace allows us to understand:

—that our own lives are important, but our problems are not the only things to be considered:

—that there are things we can do to help, but we must rely on God in the final analysis:

—that we always have help and comfort through his Spirit. Perhaps H. Reinhold Niebuhr has put it best:

> God grant me the serenity to accept
>   the things I cannot change,
> The courage to change
>   the things I can,
> And the wisdom to know the difference.

Joy in Christ
4:10-12

In my life in union with the Lord is a great joy to me that after so long a time you once more had the chance of showing that you care for me. I don't mean that you had stopped caring for me—you just had no chance to show it. And I am not saying this because I feel neglected, for I have learned to be satisfied with what I have. I know what it is to be in need and what it is to have more than enough. I have learned this secret, so that anywhere, at any time, I am content, whether I am full or hungry, whether I have too much or too little (4:10-12, GNB).

"Happiness turns up more or less where you'd expect it to—a good marriage, a rewarding job, a pleasant vacation. Joy, on the other hand, is as notoriously unpredictable as the one who bequeathes it."[5]

The older I get, the more I'm convinced that there is a great difference between happiness and joy. People struggle to find happiness in life. Happiness is a kind of commodity in that sense. Living life joyfully, on the other hand, is not the end of the journey—not that which is attained at the end of the search. It is the celebration of the journey itself. If you found a pot of gold at the rainbow's end, you'd be happy. But a joyful person would marvel at the colors of the rainbow along the way. The joyful person might get so caught up in the rainbow that he forgets to hurry to the end. He might even think reds, blues, and greens are prettier than gold anyway.

Joy is a perspective, a lens for viewing life. Joy is childlike. But for Jesus, it is the only attitude that matters. Joy is the celebration of life. Joy often doesn't ask why, though it is not blind, as much as it confesses the glory of what is. And that confession of joy comes through statement, through tears, and through laughter.[6]

Joy is expressed in confession, through testimony and witness. That what I have, however much, is enough. That's because I have the Son, or rather because he has me, I may rest in his care for me. Joy is the confession of God's love toward us all in general, to each of us in particular.

Joy is seen in tears, too. Joy and tears are not mutually exclusive. Tears express greater joy than smiles. Tears as the joy of pride. Tears as the joy of love. Tears express the unspeakable joy of God's love, joy which can sometimes be expressed no other way.

Joy is expressed in laughter. The laughter of little children and old women. The unpretentious laughter of good friends as they share the joy of fellowship. You may forget the place, the time, or the occasion. But you never forget the confession, the tears, or the laughter. The joy endures.

Joy is like my nephew and the trash can. One day, while he was a creeper, he saw my mother put something into the trash can. It was one of those kinds in which the lid spun around if you hit it hard enough. She did. It spun. Bill laughed so hard that he shook. Laughing till he shook—over the discovery of a trash can—of such is the kingdom of God.

Holy Father,
We pray to confess you as our maker and
    Redeemer,
Crying and laughing—not from want or
    silliness—but for joy.
Help us enjoy the rainbow's colors, as well as the

promise of gold.

Enable us to confess. Help us cry. Inspire our laughter.

As we make joy our way of viewing life.

Through Christ,
Amen.

Partners in the Gospel
4:14-17

But it was very good of you to help me in my troubles. You Philippians know very well that when I left Macedonia, in the early days of preaching the Good News, you were the only church to help me; you were the only ones who shared my profits and losses. More than once when I needed help in Thessalonica, you sent it to me. It is not that I just want to receive gifts; rather, I want to see profit added to your account (4:14-17, GNB).

"Let's not be too quick to criticize. After all, we're all in this thing together," my coach said one Saturday. We had been bickering over a double-play ball that had been missed. But we still had the rest of the game to worry about. The coach encouraged us to pull together as a team.

We were a team. Partners. We had to play together—pull each other up, make up for each other's mistakes. We were not players for our individual selves. We were all in the game together.

What was true for our ball team is true for our fellowship in the faith. We have this one calling among us. And we work together for the one calling of Christ. We're partners.

For Paul and the Philippian church, their partnership included financial and spiritual support. And as Philippi shared in the expenses of Paul's journey, Philippi also gained credit for the work done. Paul could not have done what he did without their support.

But that's what being partners is about. With partners:

—What happens to one automatically affects the other. In another place, Paul said that if one member of the body suffers, all members suffer.

—If one prospers, all prosper.

—The partnership occurs on various levels. Financially, prayerfully, actually helping in the work itself.

—The involvement is personal—people with people. And our investment is an investment of ourselves.

In all of life, we are known by association—by the company we keep. But too often, we let the "fellowship of the saints" exist apart from our worship days and special events. And that's sad. Christians ought to acknowledge their partnership with others, their need for others, and then act on it.

In fellowship with other Christians we will find support, strength, goodwill, and a place to be.

Once a young English preacher was talking to an older minister at the senior minister's house. As they sat before the fire, the young preacher asked if the older minister did not think it possible for Christianity to be lived in isolation—apart from the church and the fellowship of the saints. The senior minister did not speak but took the tongs lying beside the hearth, removed a coal from the blaze, and placed it onto the hearth. The coal soon cooled and died.

There is strength in our fellowship. There is decay if we do not take advantage of the support of the church. Paul found strength in community with the Philippians church. We may find strength with all those Christians around us.

Father,
Help me support other Christians,
Even as I try to find support in your body.
Give me strength so that others will lean on me.
Help me be willing to lean on others.
For we are all in this thing together.
Partners—by choice, by grace, through Christ.

Amen.

Glory to God
4:20

To our God and Father be all the glory forever and ever! Amen (4:20, GNB).

The angels over the Bethlehem field that night certainly didn't say it first. But perhaps they said it best.

"And suddenly there was with the angel a multitude of the heavenly host praising God and saying,

'Glory to God in the highest,
and on earth peace among men with whom
he is pleased!'" (Luke 2:13-14, RSV).

Powerfully, majestically, and musically they sang "Glory to God!"

Knowingly, wisely, and through grace Paul said, "To the only wise God be glory for evermore" (Rom. 16:27, RSV).

Even my father said it. Not as beautifully as the angels, to be sure. Probably not even with the sureness or understanding of Paul. But before and after each service he preached, he prayed "And we'll be careful to give you all the glory, O God, our Father.''

Dear Lord, why can't I say it?

"And what is it, child, that you cannot say to me?" spoke the Father.

Somehow, Father, I can't say "Glory to you," because I don't know exactly what it means. I mean, I know you're God, and that you're all-present, all-knowing, all-seeing, all-everything. And even all my best words don't even get close to who you really are.

"You're right."

So how can I glorify you? You're already glorified. You're already Glory itself. Nothing I say will make you more glorious than you are. Nothing I have to offer you in the way of praise is good enough, or worthy enough. The whole of creation, the whole universe proclaims your glory.

"Are you, child, not part of my creation?"

I know I am, Father. But the stars shine so brightly, and the ocean roars so deeply. The birds sing so sweetly. And all praise you. I am but a man-child. What do I have to offer in the way of praise to equal those? How can I glorify you?

"But the people of the earth are more important to me than stars, birds, or oceans—though all of my work is important. Yet man alone is worth dying for. All else worships for they cannot do otherwise. Only you, child, are free to love me or not to love me. You may glorify me more than all the others together."

But Father, all I can offer to you is me.

"And because I am your God, and your Father, that is enough."

Then, O Lord, I give myself to you as the only praise I may give. I acknowledge your greatness and glory. I proclaim your wonder. But I love you because you want me for your own. All I am shall be yours forever more.

"We shall both know the glory of this moment, child. Now, and forever."

Amen.

"Amen."

Greetings and Grace
4:21-23

Greetings to each one of God's people who belong to Christ Jesus. The brothers here with me send you their greetings. All God's people here send greetings, especially those who belong to the Emperor's palace. May the grace of the Lord Jesus Christ be with you all (4:21-23, GNB).

I heard a lady preacher on the gospel radio station one day. And she was letting it fly. She was especially getting on to people who made fun of her ministry. She remembered Jeremiah 48, where God had cursed Moab (vv. 35 ff.), and she said, "Through the Lord Jesus Christ I curse you with the curse of baldness. All of you who laugh at me and my ministry shall be bald. Thank you, Jesus!" She cursed those folks over the radio! And in the name of Jesus!

Now do you think that's right? The curse, I mean.

Now the curse has always been a big part of superstition. People who are superstitious have to really watch their steps or they'll get zapped with a curse of one kind or another, bad luck and all.

But Christianity is not superstition.

However, the curse is pretty important in religion too. Prophets have pronounced curses on cities and people for a long time. And those destructive words, hurled from the marketplace or the pulpit, are the

strongest force in most religion. The curse strikes
fear in the heart of the hearer. Fear of hell, of baldness, of pestilence, of illness. Curses cause fear. And
that fear is strong. That lady preacher meant to
frighten her detractors. Not only that, she probably
prayed for those folks' hair to fall out. Vengeance.
Curse. And in the name of Christ. Know any Christians—even preachers—like that, "cursing" in the
name of Christ?

I feel sorry for that lady preacher, and for all those
like her who preach curses. I'm sorrier for those who
bother to listen and who take them seriously enough
to be afraid. For while in some religious understand-
ings the "curse" of God may be paramount, the
major message the Son of God preaches is that the
curse has been taken away! No more fear! No more
shame! No more need to walk in dread—of baldness
or whatever!

No. Jesus tells us of God's love. That love casts
out our fear. Read 1 John 4, especially v. 18.

And not only fear. Love casts out malice and hate.
Love doesn't let us curse our neighbor. God's love,
when we allow it to be lord of our life, keeps us from
wanting the bad for anyone. We want to bless others
because we've been blessed. We've experienced the
love of God, and we want others to experience it as
well.

I could be wrong, but it seems to me that there are
some sincere folk who would like to see hell swallow
up the world so they can be proven "right." They
want vengeance to be paid to those unbelievers for
their cruel words, laughter, and inattention.

Jesus, however, did not laugh vindictively at Jerusalem. He wept over the city. He loved the people.
Judgment for him was not joy in cursing people for
not believing him so he would be proven right. Jesus

would have much rather blessed Jerusalem.

So should we. We should be willing to bless, to redeem in action and word, to love. Any religion can "curse." Only Christians, because of our encounter with Jesus, can truly bless.

Paul blessed those to whom he wrote. He opened and closed his correspondence with blessings. We should strive, through the love of God through the Lord Jesus Christ, to bless those with whom we come into contact. To bless those around us—believers or not—to show love, not hate. To show mercy, not vengeance. To show giving, not demanding. To show grace.

Blessings to all. Through Christ our Lord.
Father,
Help us live a blessed and blessing life,
A life of praise to God, and favor to our
    neighbors.
Help us bless you and each other,
Even as we love all persons through the Son of
    your love.

Through Christ our Lord,
Amen.

And now may the love of the Father of our Lord Jesus Christ be with you all forever. May the pages of Scripture hold new truth for you. May the joy and peace of our Lord, the fellowship of the saints, and the leading of the Spirit abide in you, comfort you, and direct all your paths. Through Christ our Lord,
Amen.

Notes

Section II

1. C. S. Lewis, *The Last Battle* (New York: Macmillan, 1956), pp. 70-71.

2. Ibid., p. 136.

3. Richard Banks in *Quote, Unquote,* compiler Lloyd Corey (Wheaton, Ill.: Victor Book, Div. of SP, 1977), p.112-115.

4. Helmut Thielicke, *The Waiting Father* (Scranton, Pa.: Harper and Row, 1959), p. 62.

5. Ibid.

6. Frederick Buechner, *Wishful Thinking* (Scranton, Pa.: Harper Religious Books, 1973), p. 47.

Section III

1. Isaac Beches in *Mead's Encyclopedia of Religious Quotations* (Westwood, N.J.: Fleming H. Revell, 1965), p. 76.

2. Ibid., p. 77.

3. Ibid.

4. Ibid., p. 75.

5. Buechner, p. 47.

6. Frederick Buechner, *Alphabet of Grace* (Fredrick, N.Y.: Seaburg Press, 1977), p. 44.